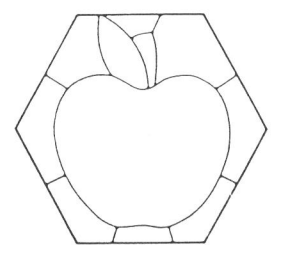

Easy-to-Make STAINED GLASS CANDLE SHELTERS

With Full-Size Templates

Ed Sibbett, Jr.

DOVER PUBLICATIONS, INC.
New York

Copyright © 1984 by Ed Sibbett, Jr.
All rights reserved under Pan American and International Copyright Conventions.

Published in Canada by General Publishing Company, Ltd., 30 Lesmill Road, Don Mills, Toronto, Ontario.

Published in the United Kingdom by Constable and Company, Ltd., 10 Orange Street, London WC2H 7EG.

Easy-to-Make Stained Glass Candle Shelters: With Full-Size Templates is a new work, first published by Dover Publications, Inc., in 1984.

Manufactured in the United States of America
Dover Publications, Inc., 31 East 2nd Street, Mineola, N.Y. 11501

Library of Congress Cataloging in Publication Data

Sibbett, Ed.
   Easy-to-make stained glass candle shelters.

   1. Glass craft—Patterns. 2. Glass painting and staining—Patterns. I. Title. II. Title: Candle shelters.
TT298.S488   1984   749'.63   83-20572
ISBN 0-486-24668-X

INTRODUCTION

Flickering candles glow to greatest advantage when their light is refracted through decorative enclosures of stained glass, mirrors and glass jewels. In this collection of candle shelter templates, Ed Sibbett, Jr. has provided over forty designs featuring attractive floral, geometric, butterfly, swan, sun, star and cathedral window motifs. The completed works make exemplary display items and are truly gifts for all seasons.

These candle shelter patterns comprise a variety of shapes and designs. The choices include open-faced, two-sided, platform-bottomed shelters that leave the candle in view and four- or five-sided types that partially or completely enclose the candle and may or may not have a bottom or platform base. Figures A through H show how some of the more complex shelters are constructed. The patterns can be altered; you may, for example, wish to use the front panel four times instead of a front, back and two sides. Bottoms and platform bases are included in only a few of the patterns, but bottoms may be added to a shelter if you want a box-like structure. Bottoms are often made from mirror glass. The square and round glass jewels shown in six of the patterns are optional. Sections that are the right size for glass jewels have been included in some patterns, such as those on Plate 1.

These projects are intended for craftspeople already familiar with the basics of the craft, but directions are included for copper foiling and for special pattern features. For more extensive instructions on stained glass work you may wish to refer to one of the introductions to the field, such as *Stained Glass Craft* by J. A. F. Divine and G. Blachford, Dover Publications, 0-486-22812-6.

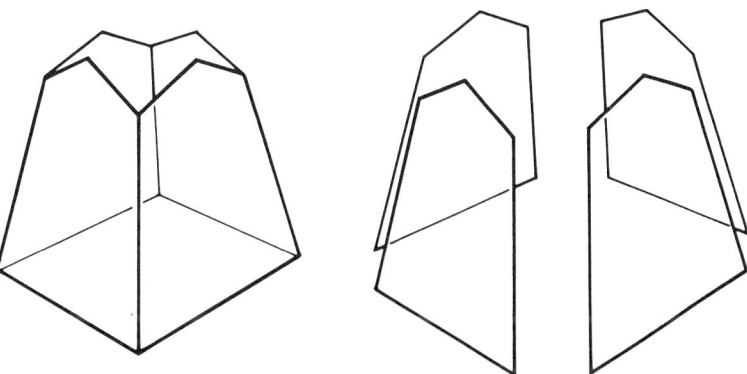

Figure A

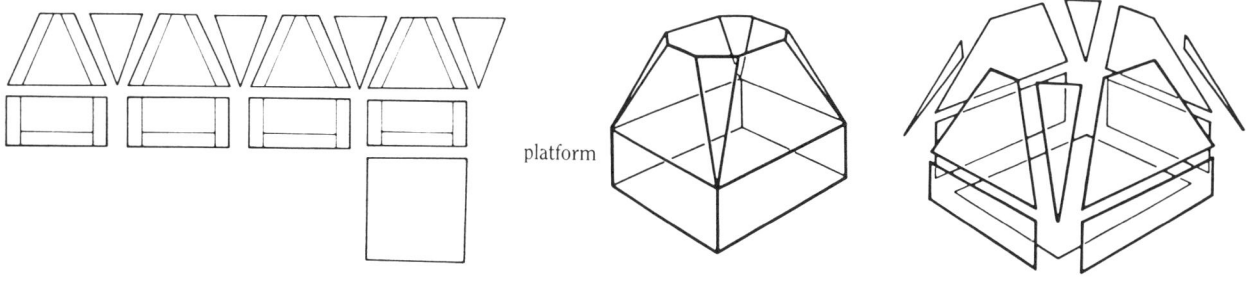

Figure B

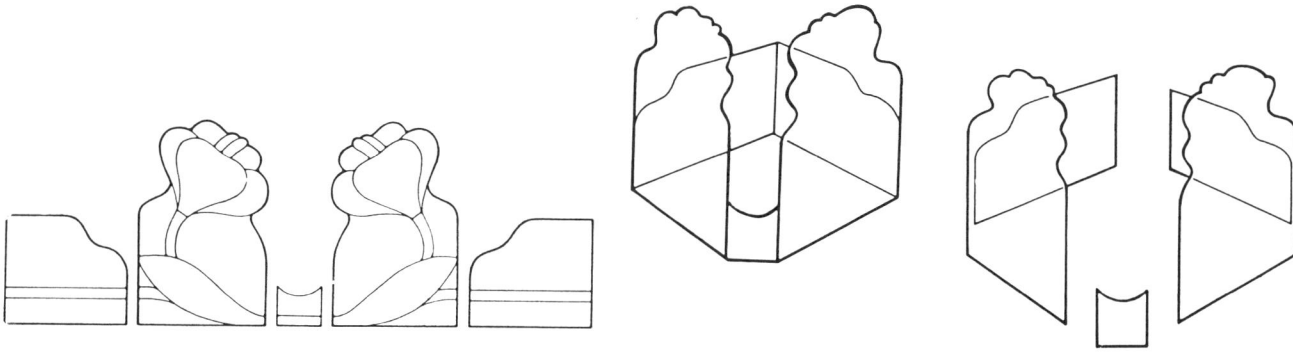

Figure C

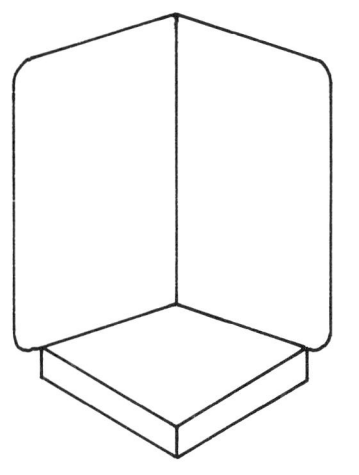

Figure D

How to Use the Templates

The patterns are numbered 1 through 42 in the order that they appear on the plates. The labels next to the templates give the pattern number and function of the panel. Use each pattern template once for the candle shelter unless, as is usually the case, the directions on the plates tell you to make repeats.

It is important to keep the edges of the heavyweight paper as neat and firm as possible, so use very sharp scissors or an X-ACTO knife when cutting out a template (you may want to remove the entire page from the book). *Trace the template onto a sheet of tracing paper before cutting the template into individual pieces.* The tracing is then used as a reference when the time comes to assemble the pieces to form a candle shelter panel. Number the pieces on the template and on the tracing. Make a rendering of your design with the colors you want to use and designate a type of glass for each section of the templates.

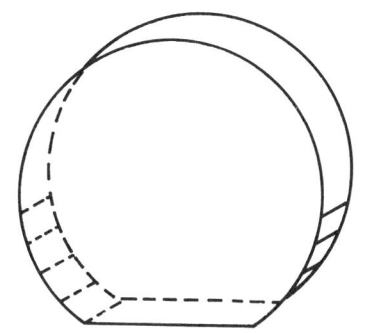

Figure E

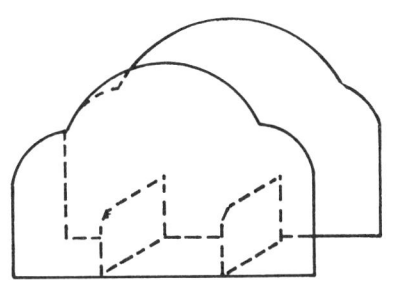

Figure F

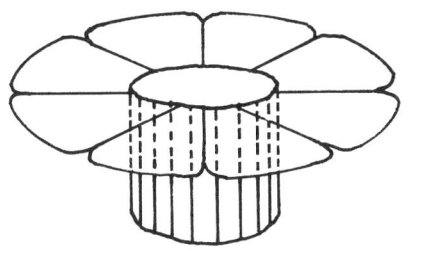

Figure G

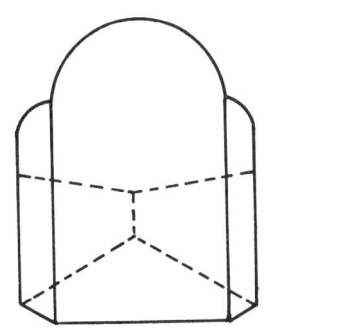

Figure H

Copper Foil Technique

After cutting the glass sections and cleaning them of oil, assemble the individual panels using the copper foil technique. Use adhesive-backed copper foil, which is available in 36-yard rolls, in widths of ³⁄₁₆″, ¼″, ⅜″ and ½″. Wrap a thin strip of foil around the edges of each glass piece. Make certain that the glass is centered over the foil so that it extends an equal distance on both sides of the glass. The foil strip should be long enough to go around all edges of the piece and overlap itself by ¼″. Press the foil carefully and firmly into place using a fid, burnisher or pencil. Trim excess foil at the corners with a scissors, razor blade or X-ACTO knife.

Fit the glass pieces of an individual panel together (the sections in the side templates of Patterns 22, 23 and 42 are separate pieces and should not be treated as a panel). Tack the corners of each piece of glass by holding a soldering iron or gun over the corners and dropping a piece of solder onto the corner. Coat the foil with a thin layer of flux and then move the soldering iron along the foil while pulling the solder close behind. On contact with the foil, the solder should melt and spread out along the entire width of the foil. Repeat this procedure with the other panels.

Assembling the Candle Shelter

When building any three-dimensional project, care must always be taken to work at a proper angle for soldering. Make sure that the solder will not merely drip down onto your working surface, but rather will flow down into the seam being joined. Prop up the object with wooden blocks or other heavy objects as shown in Figure I.

The important thing to keep in mind is that a groove should form on the outside of the juncture of two panels (see Figure J). A couple of pieces of masking tape placed perpendicular to the seam on the inside and outside are helpful in holding panels together until you have tacked them together with beads of solder at the ends of the groove.

When assembling shelters with bottoms (or platform bases), the common approach is to tack front, back and side panels to the bottom and then to each other, followed by all necessary adjustments. Once the panels are correctly aligned, flux each seam and coat with a heavy application of solder. Shelters without bottoms can simply be tacked together, side by side, and soldered. The four separate sections in the side templates in Patterns 22 and 23 should be attached around the curved edge of the front and back pieces, from bottom to halfway up the curve.

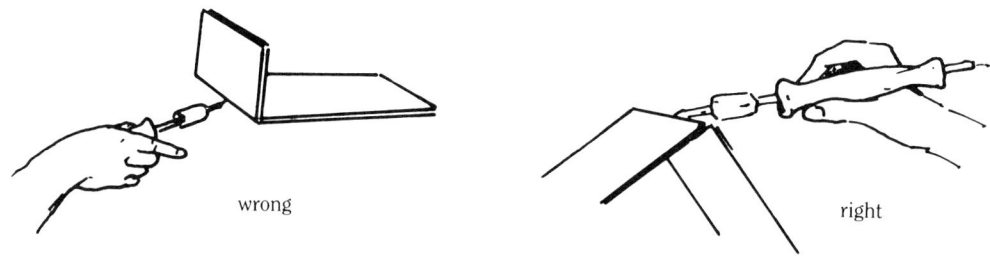

Figure I

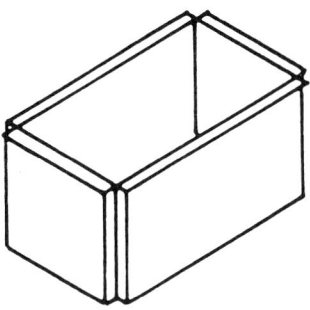

Figure J

Sources of Supply

Craft and hobby stores listed in your local yellow pages will probably have all needed materials. If supplies are unavailable, you may wish to order from one of the following businesses with national retail mail-order distribution.

Bullas Glass, Ltd., 15 Joseph Street, Kitchener, Ontario, Canada N2G 1H9
Cline Glass Co., Inc., 1135 S.E. Grand Avenue, Portland, Oregon 97214
D & L Stained Glass Supply, 4919 North Broadway, Boulder, Colorado 80302
Franciscan Glass Co., 100 San Antonio Circle, Mountain View, California 94040
Glass House Studio, Inc., 125 State Street, St. Paul, Minnesota 55107
Glassmasters Guild, 621 Avenue of the Americas, New York, New York 10011
James Hetley & Co. Ltd., Beresford Avenue, Wembley, Middlesex, HAO 1RP, England
Ed Hoy's Stained Glass, 999 East Chicago Avenue, Naperville, Illinois 60540
Hudson Glass Co., Inc., 219 D North Division Street, Peekskill, New York 10566
Nervo International, 650 University Avenue, Berkeley, California 94710
New Renaissance Glassworks, 5151 Broadway, Oakland, California 94611
Renaissance Glass Inc., 4925 Dundas Street West, Islington (Toronto), Ontario, Canada M9A 1B6
San Francisco Stained Glass Works, 3463 16th Street, San Francisco, California 94114
Stained Glass Supplies, Unit 5, Brunel Way, Thornbury Industrial Estate, Thornbury, Avon, England

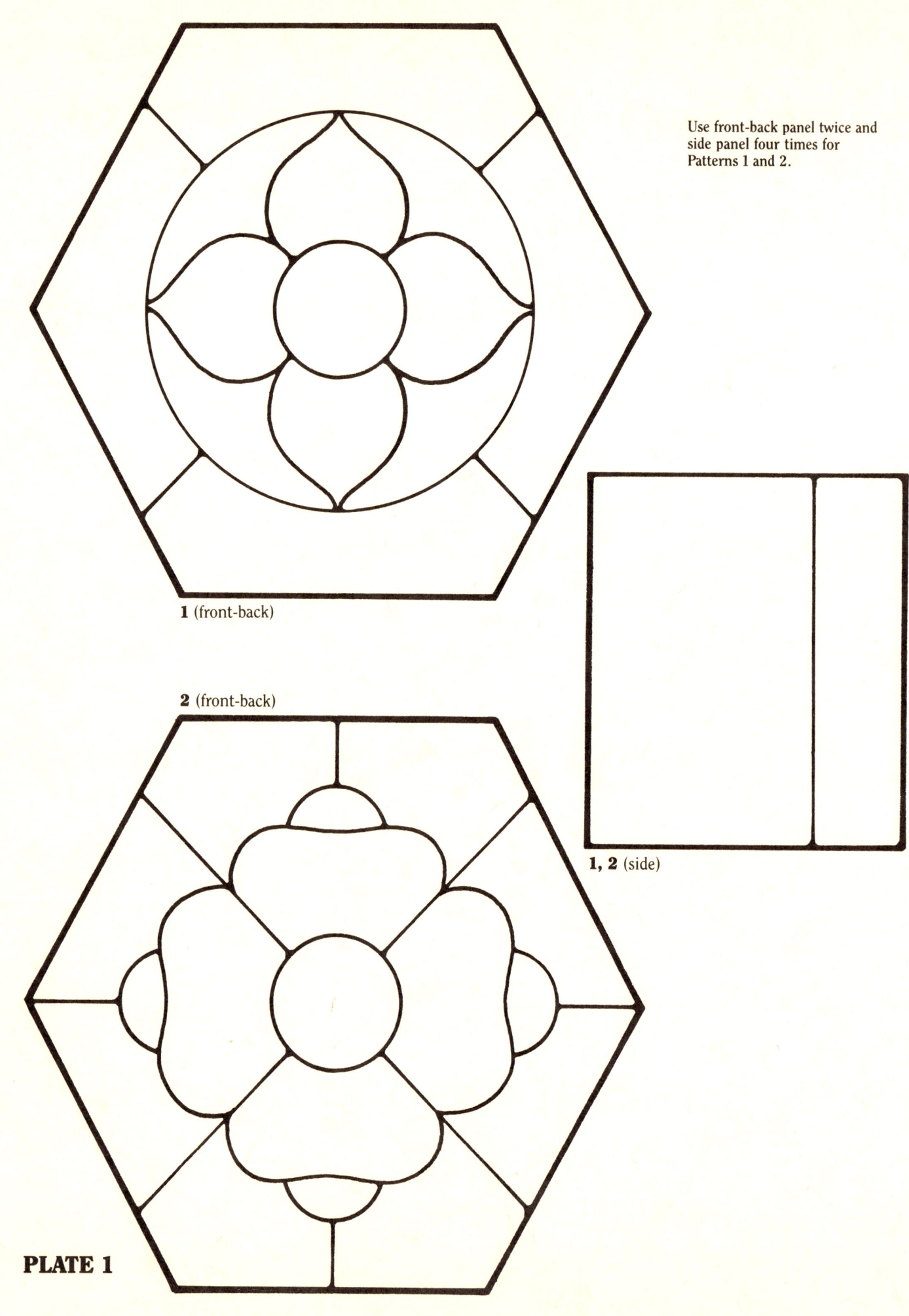

Use front-back panel twice and side panel four times for Patterns 1 and 2.

1 (front-back)

2 (front-back)

1, 2 (side)

PLATE 1

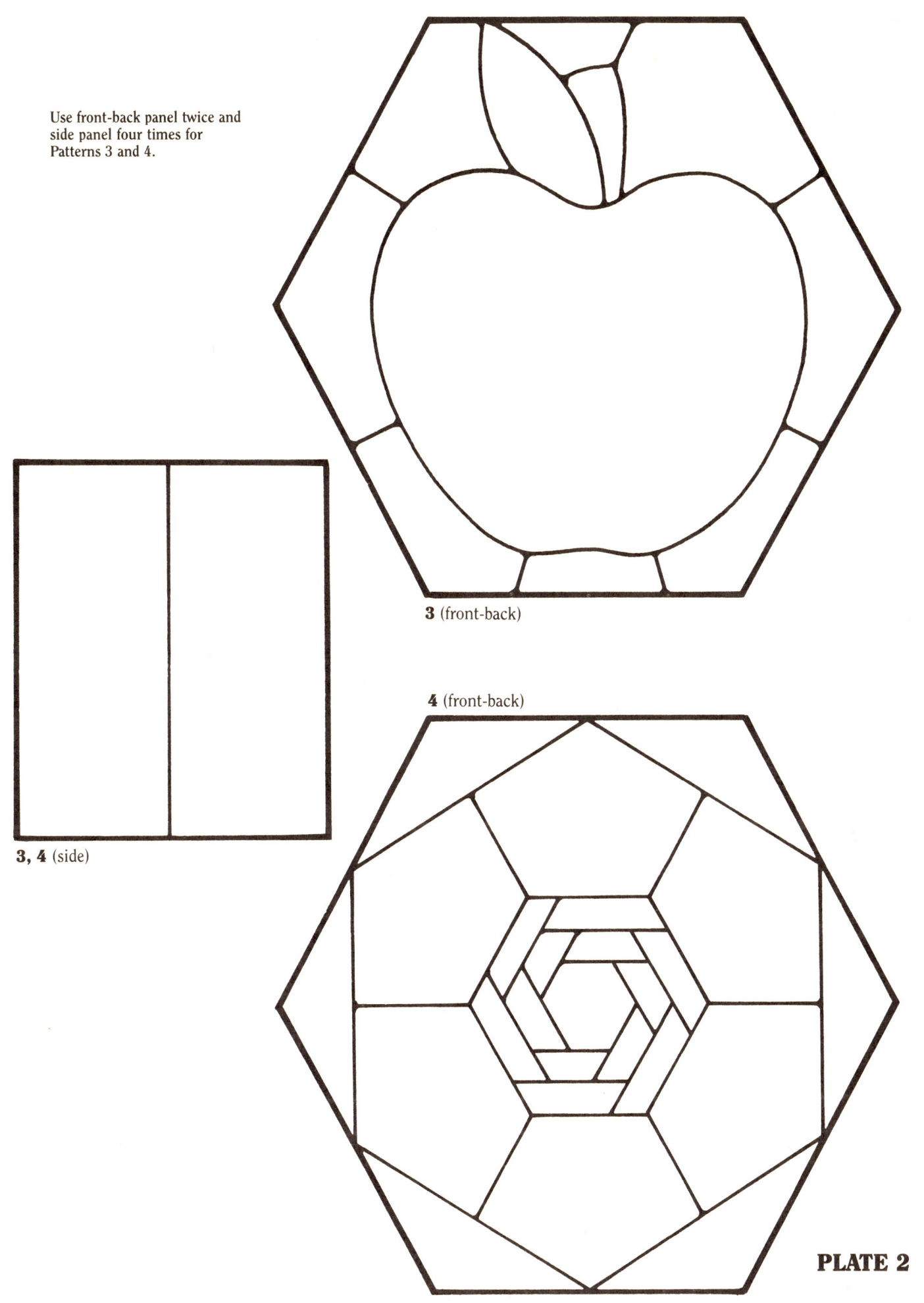

Use front-back panel twice and side panel four times for Patterns 3 and 4.

3 (front-back)

3, 4 (side)

4 (front-back)

PLATE 2

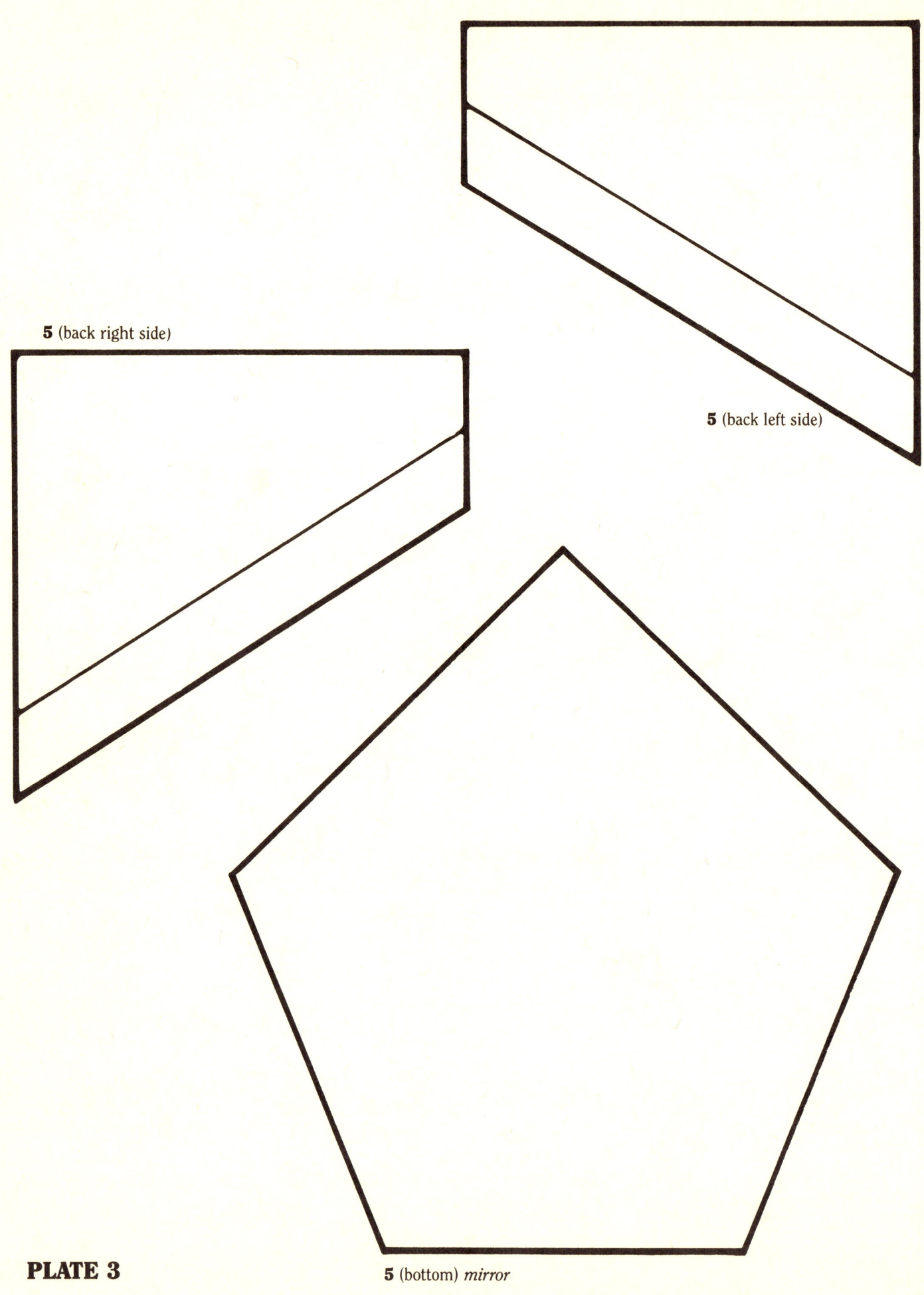

PLATE 3

5 (back right side)

5 (back left side)

5 (bottom) *mirror*

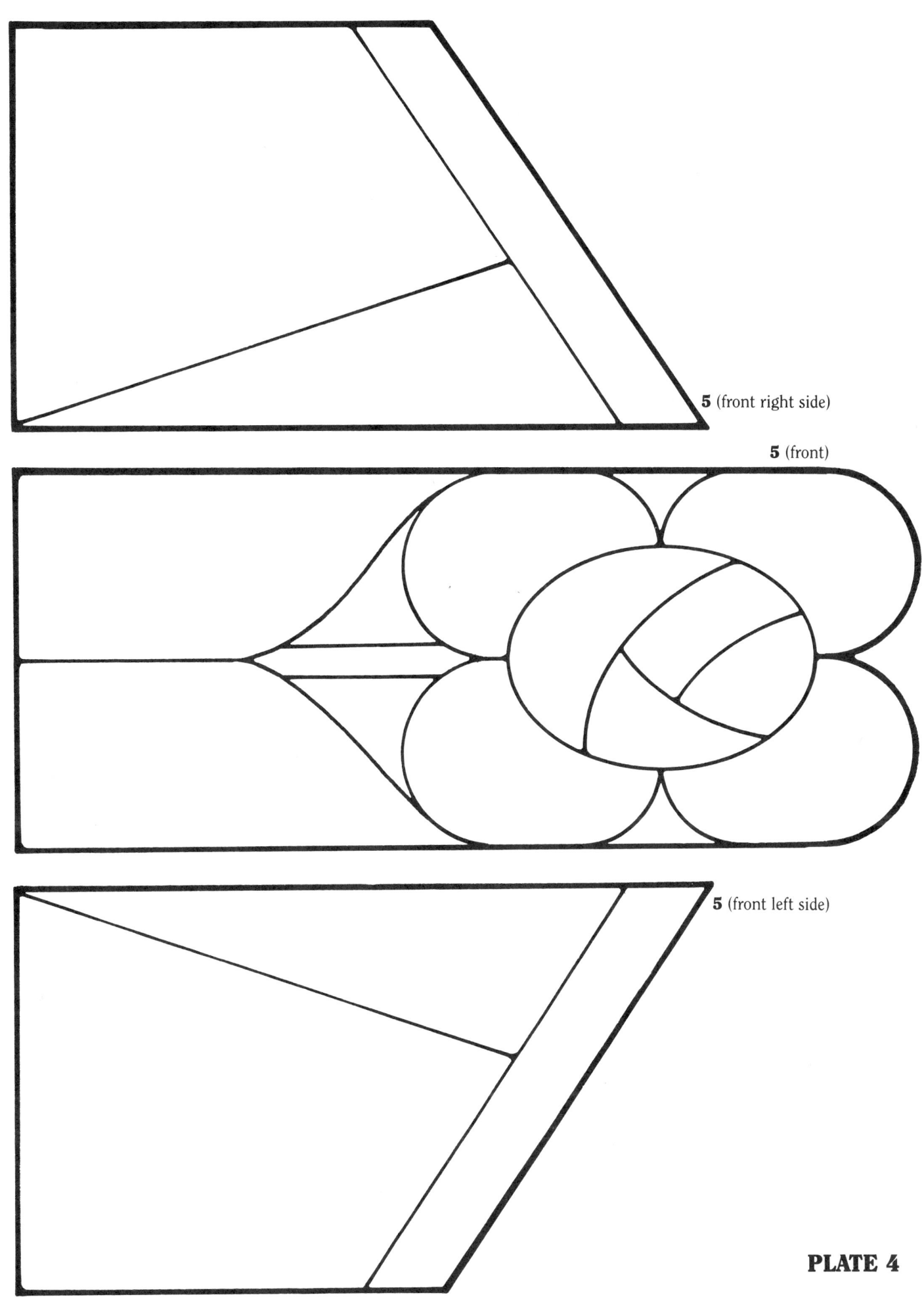

PLATE 4

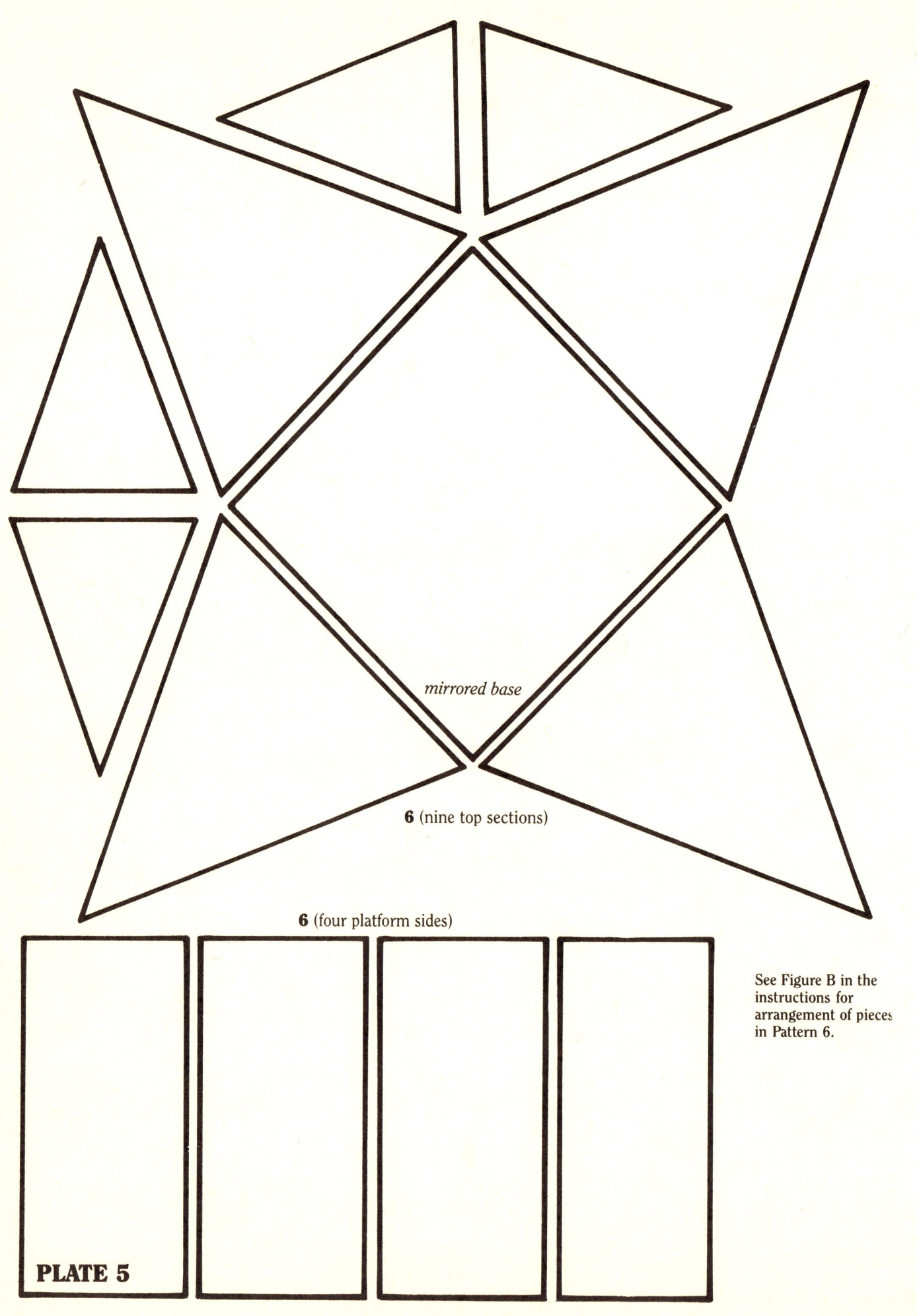

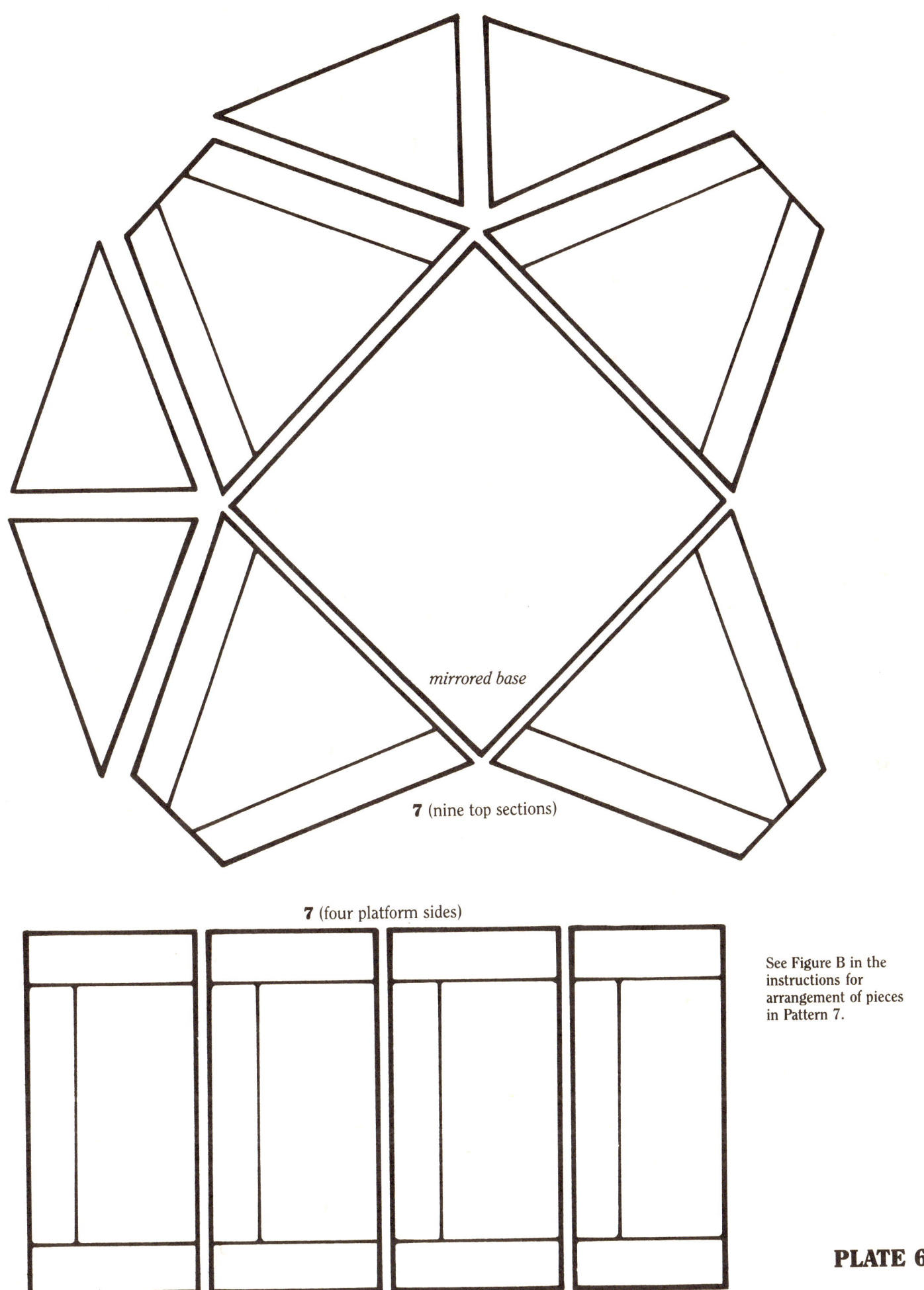

mirrored base

7 (nine top sections)

7 (four platform sides)

See Figure B in the instructions for arrangement of pieces in Pattern 7.

PLATE 6

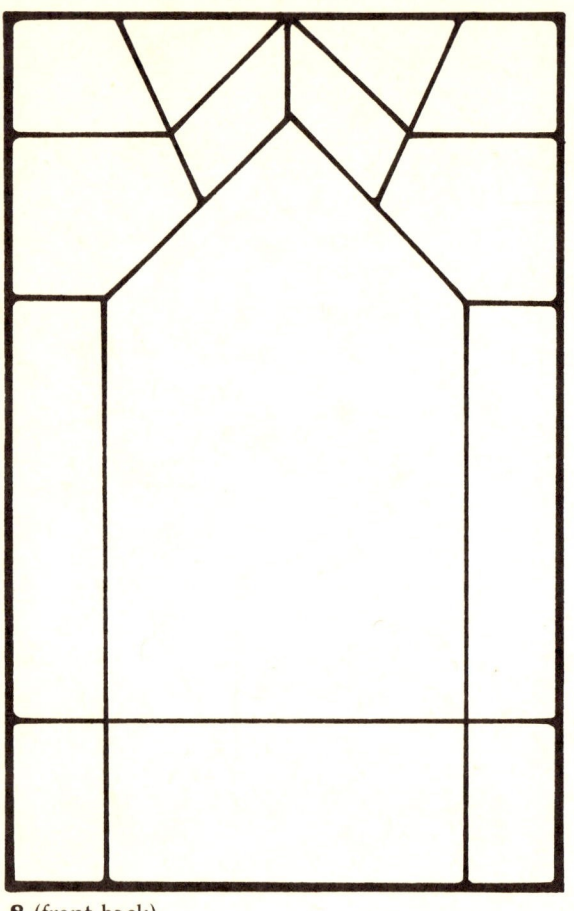

8 (front-back)

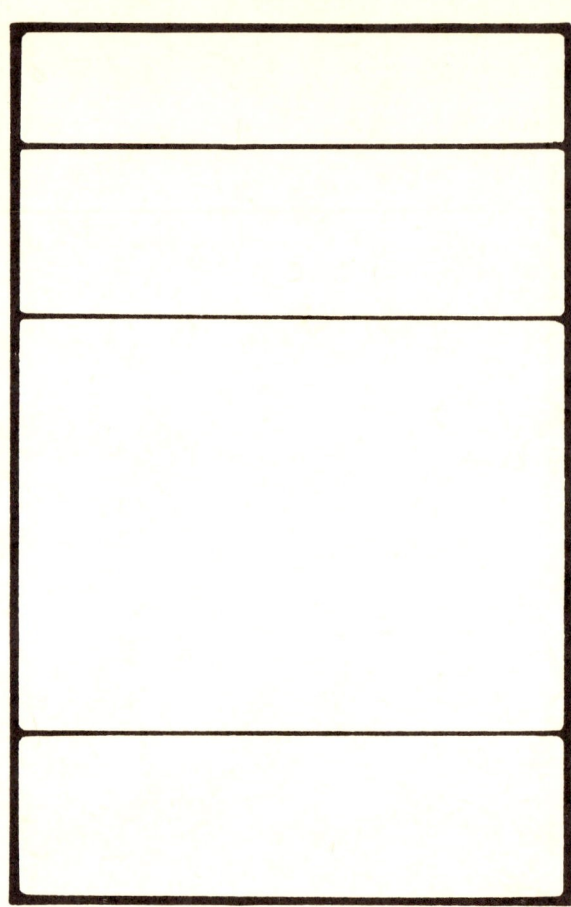

8 (side)

Use front-back and side panels twice for Patterns 8 and 9.

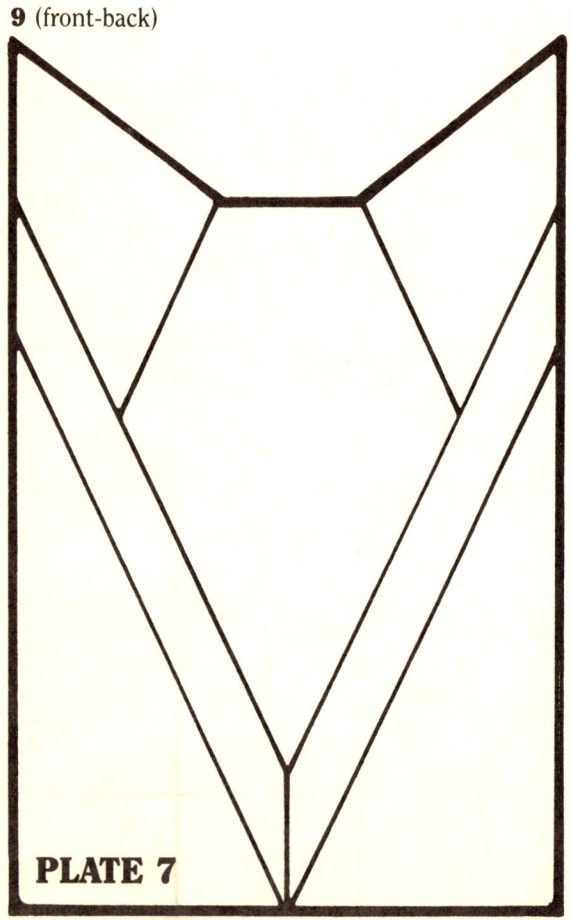

9 (front-back)

PLATE 7

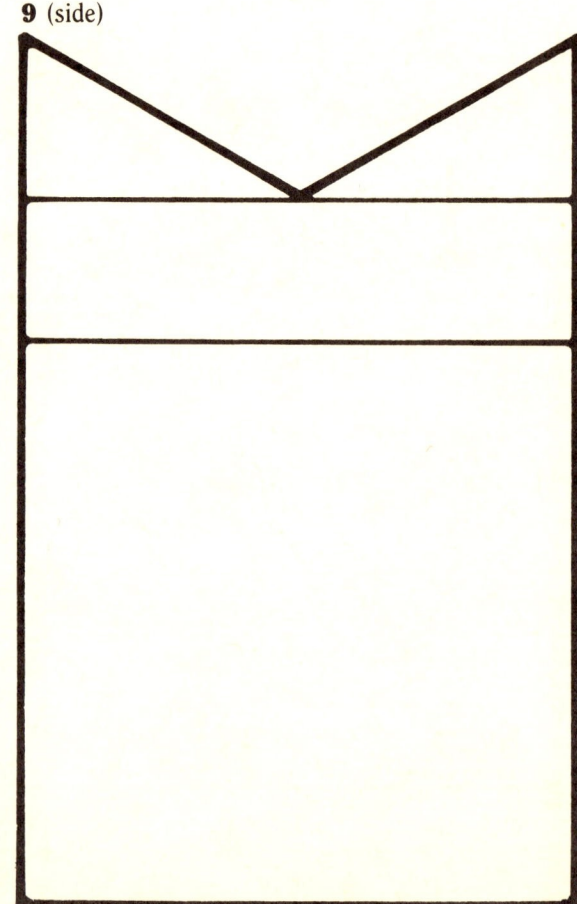

9 (side)

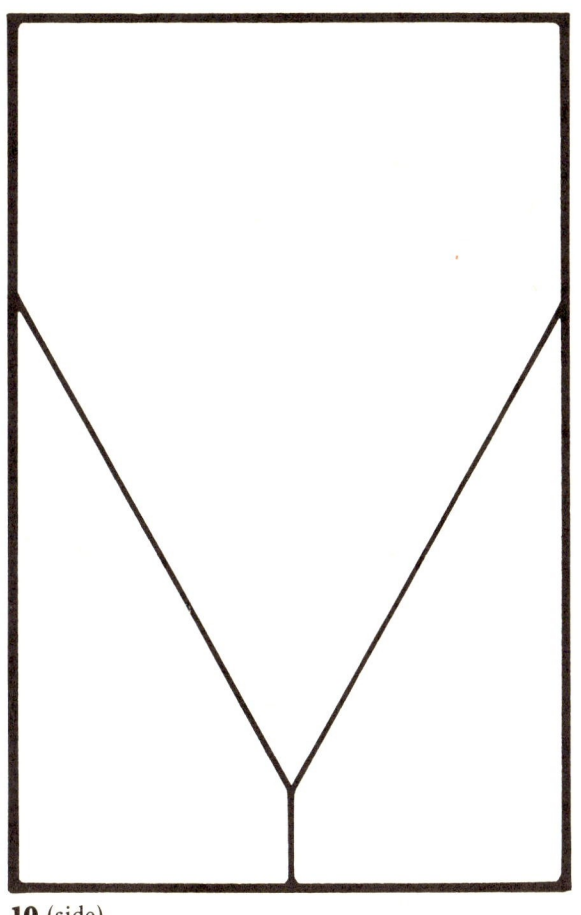
10 (side)

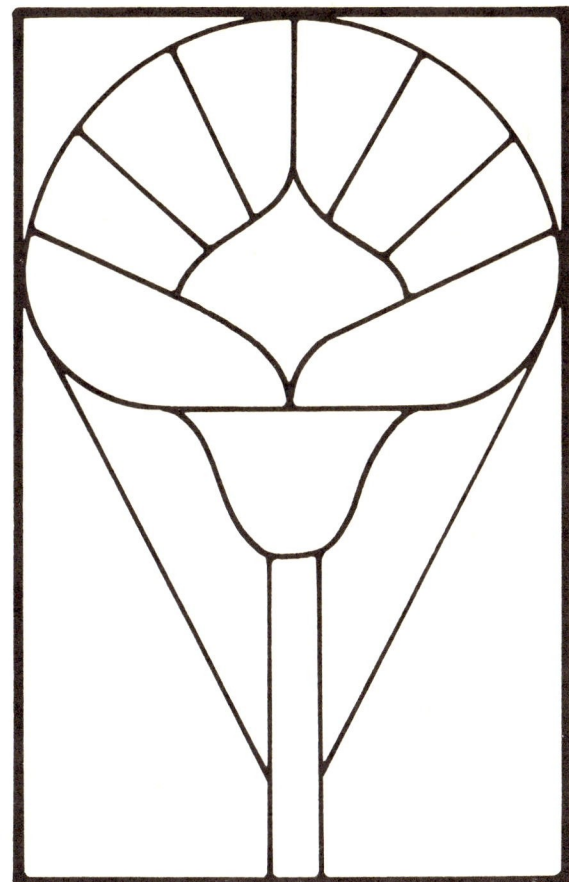
10 (front-back)

Use front-back and side panels twice for Patterns 10 and 11.

11 (side)

11 (front-back)

PLATE 8

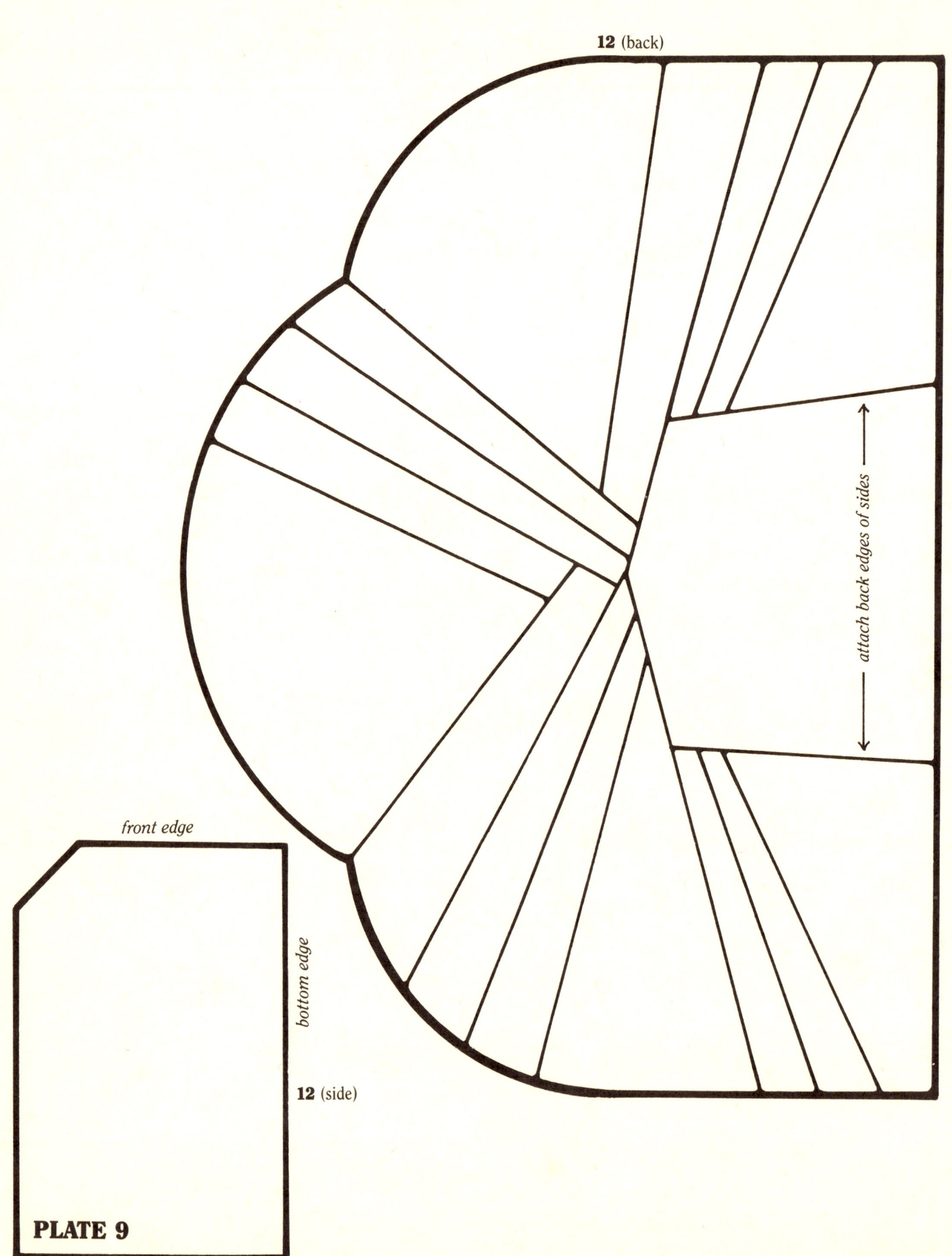

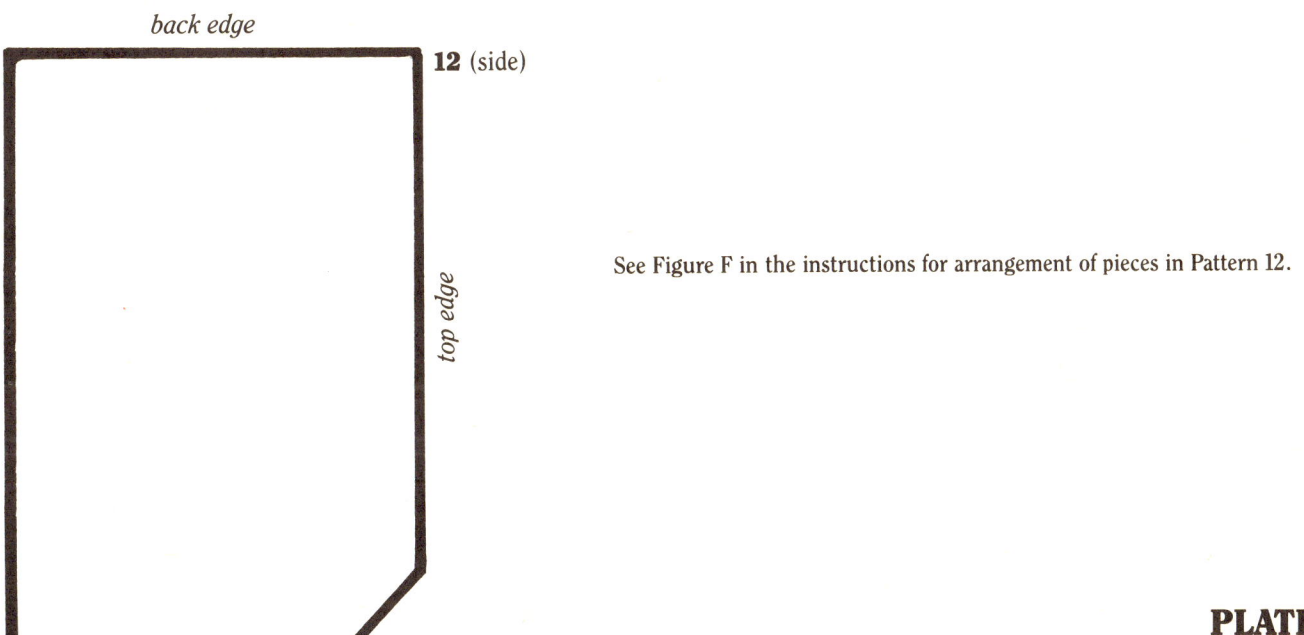

12 (front)

attach front edges of sides

back edge

12 (side)

top edge

See Figure F in the instructions for arrangement of pieces in Pattern 12.

PLATE 10

13 (front-back)

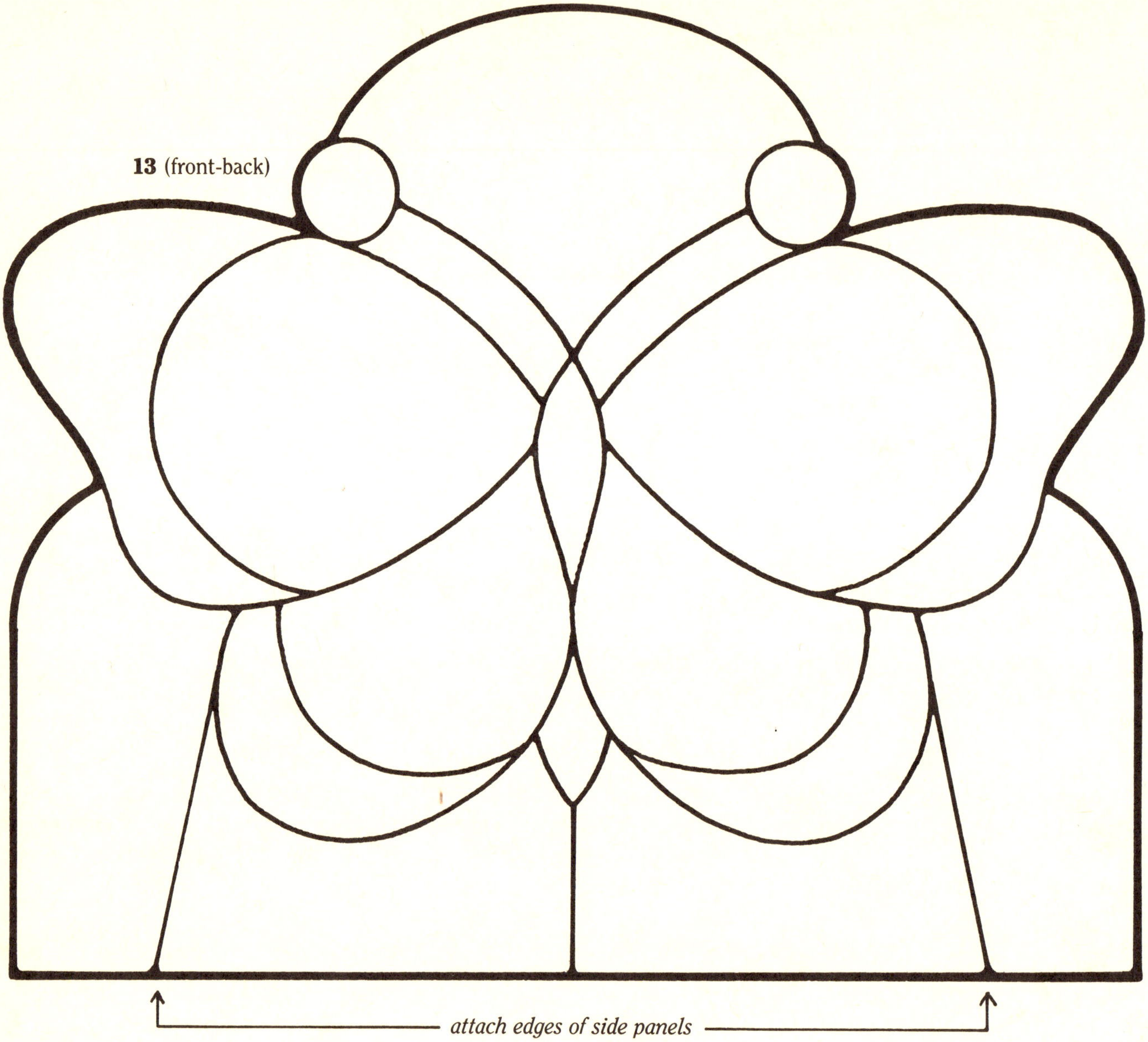

← attach edges of side panels →

Use front-back and side panels twice for Pattern 13.

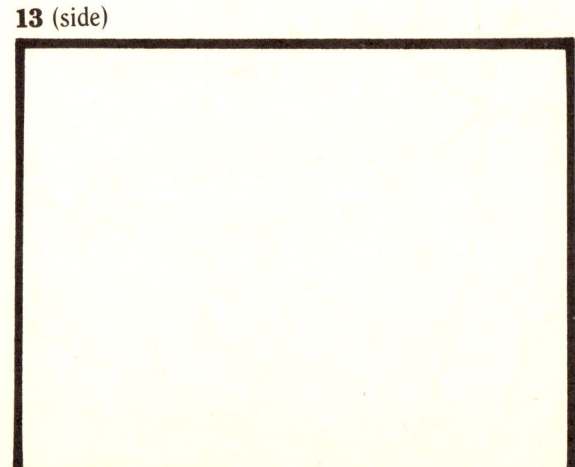

13 (side)

PLATE 11

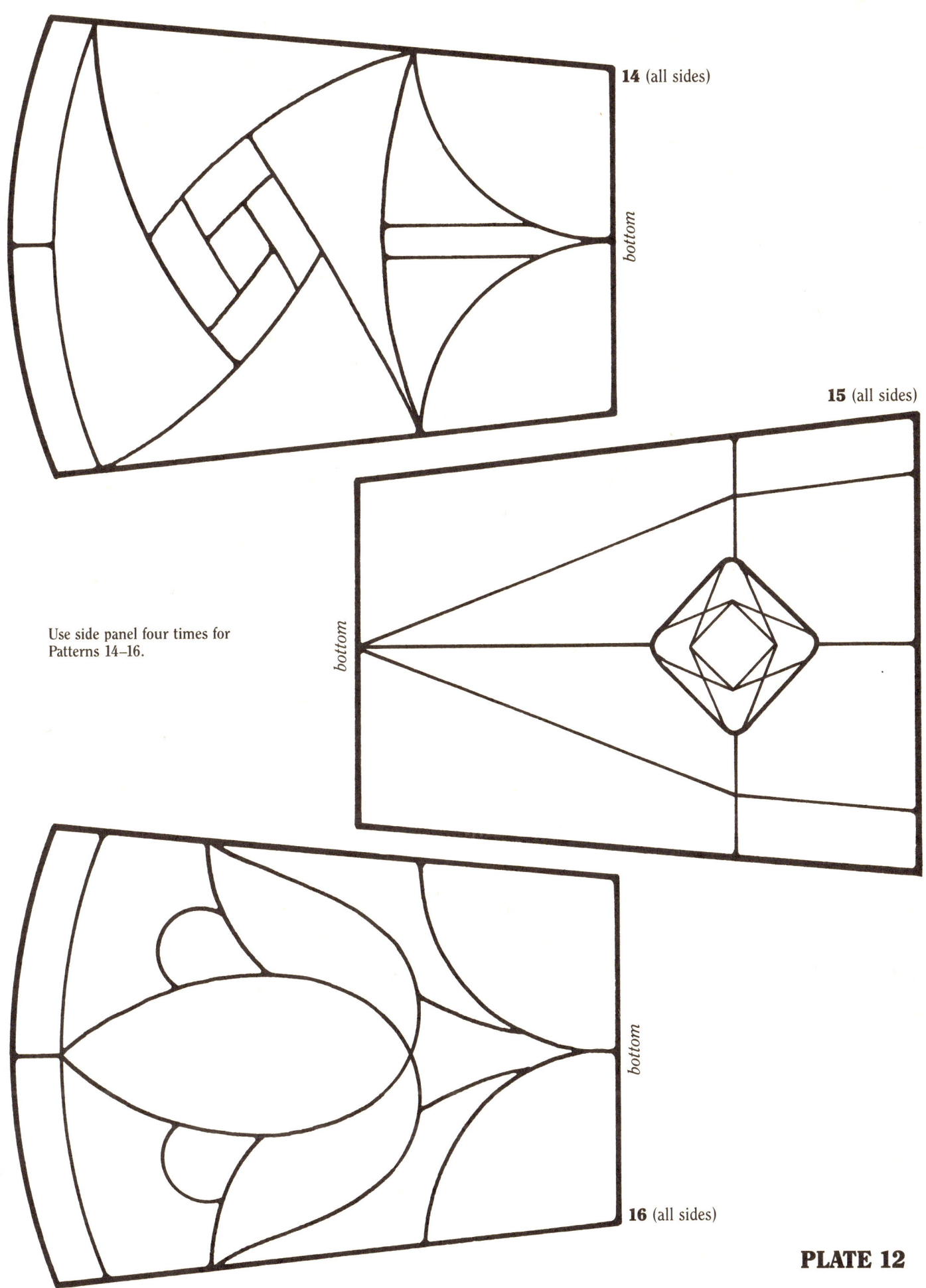

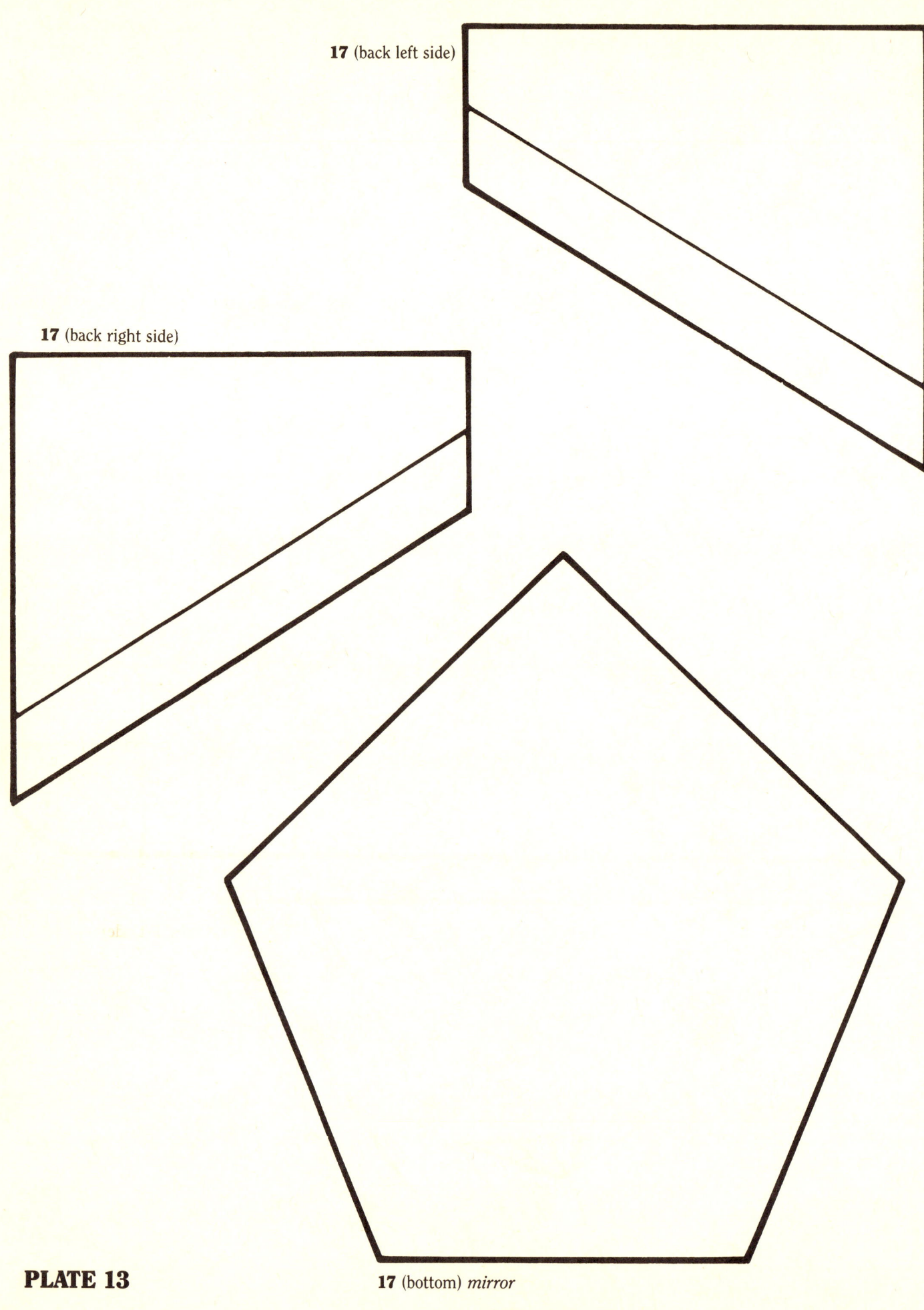

17 (back left side)

17 (back right side)

PLATE 13   **17** (bottom) *mirror*

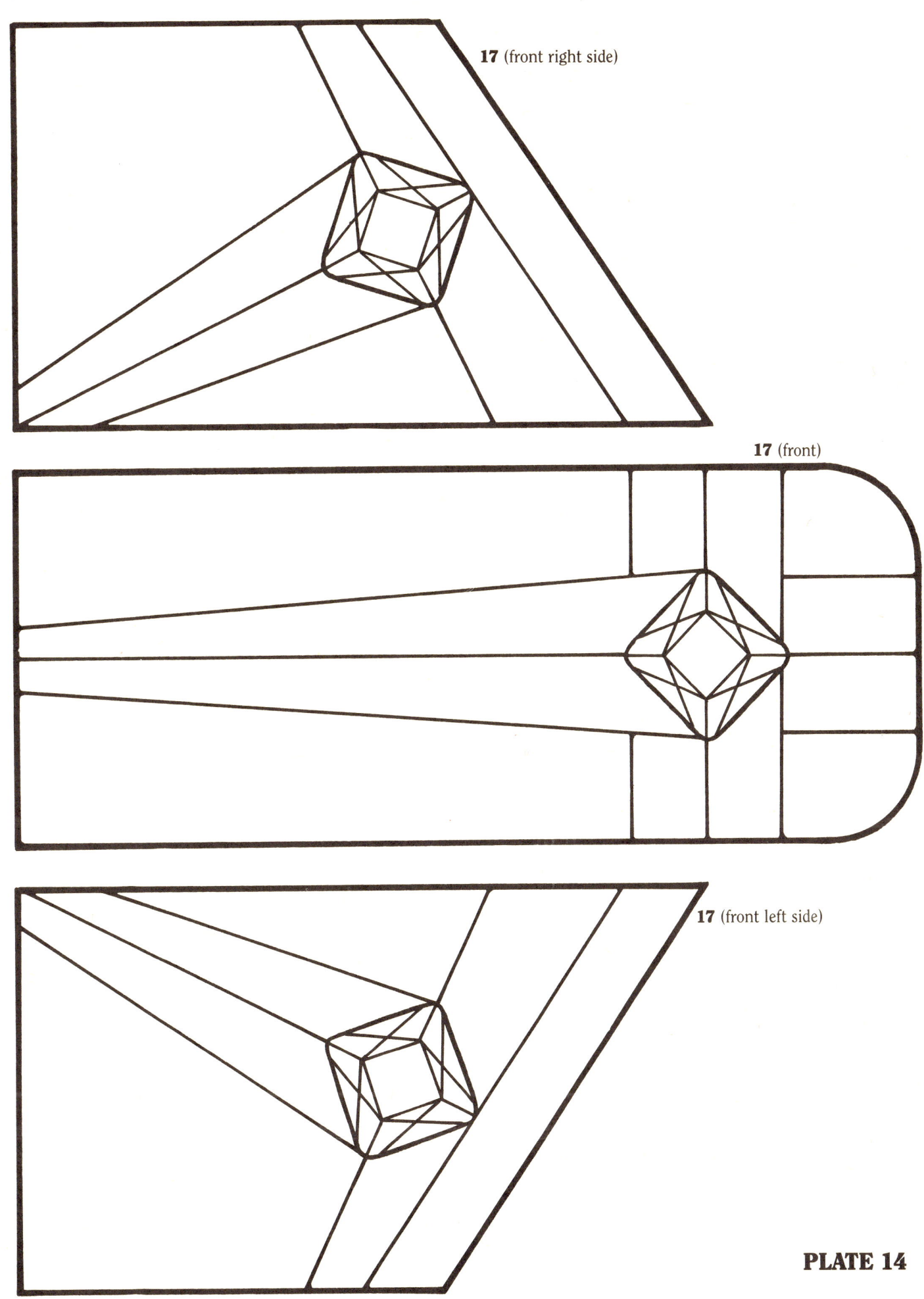

PLATE 14

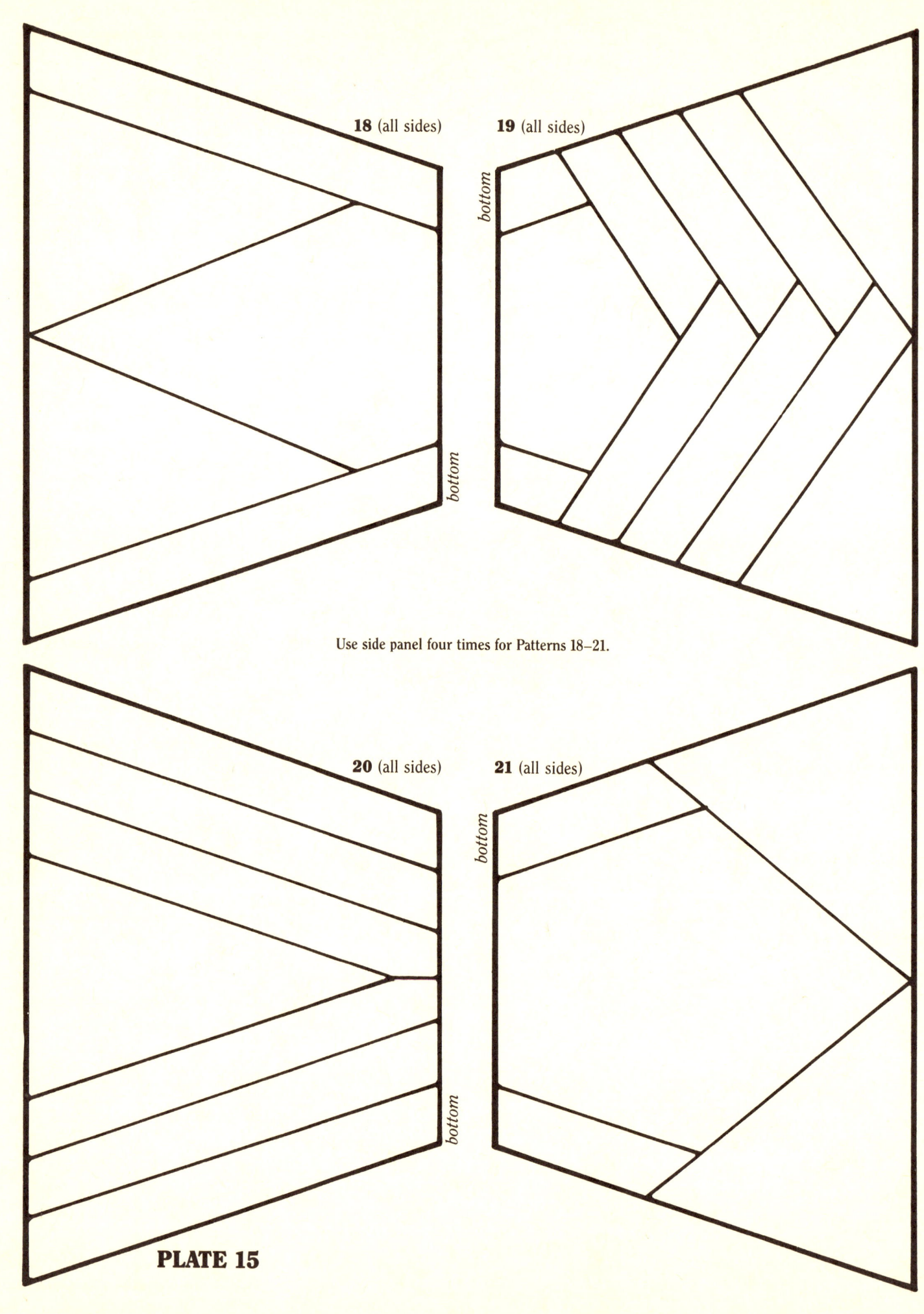

Use side panel four times for Patterns 18–21.

PLATE 15

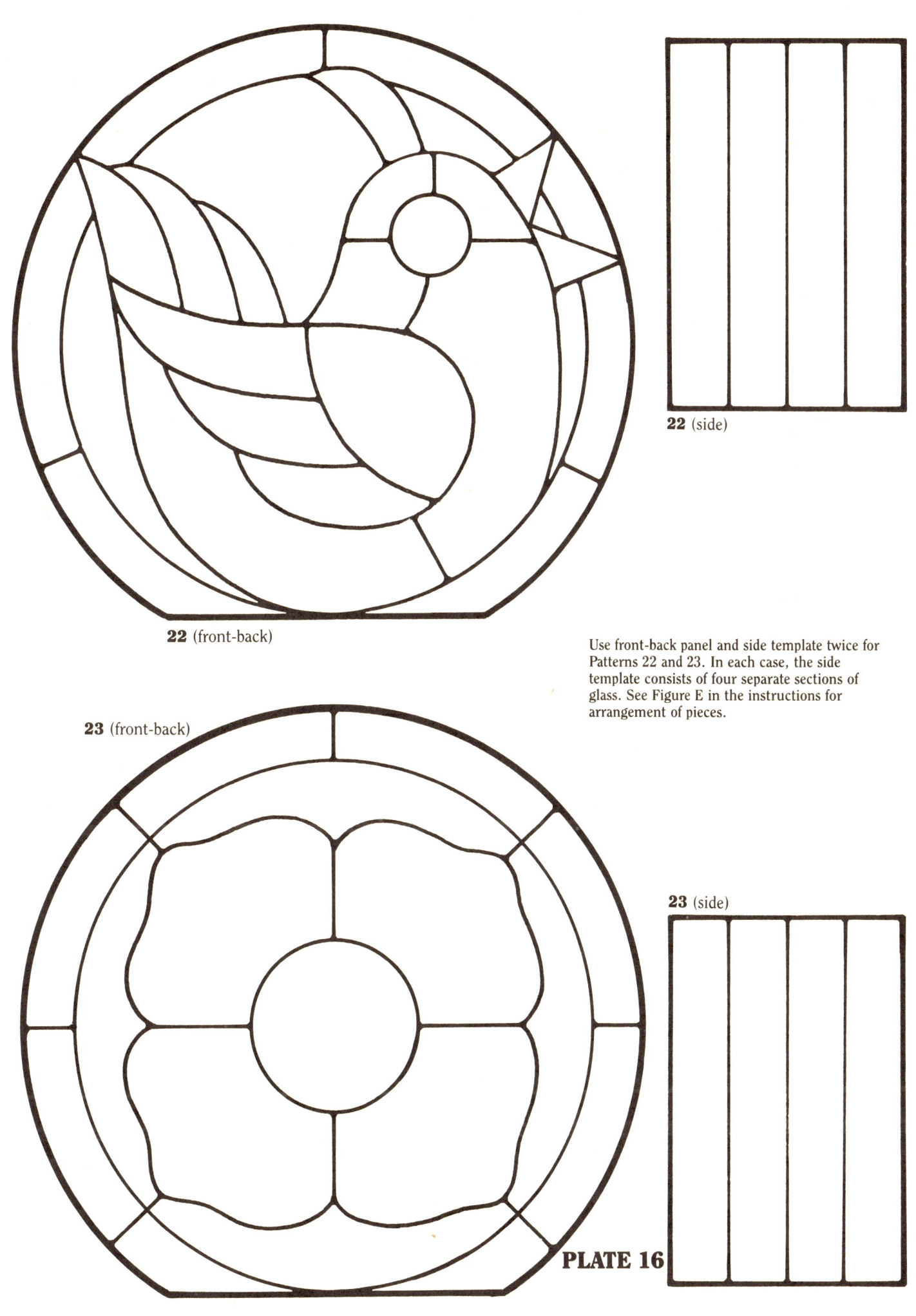

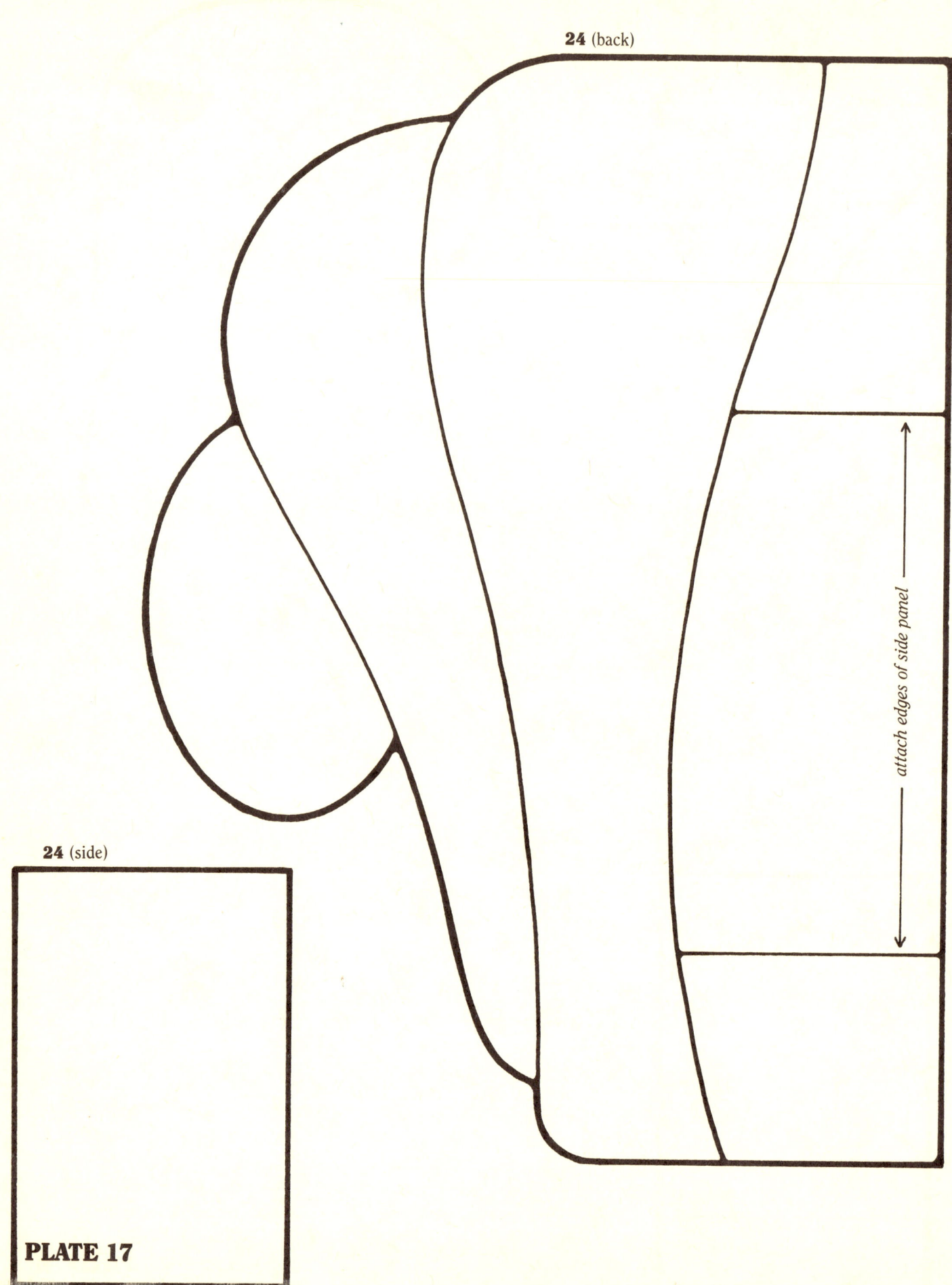

PLATE 17

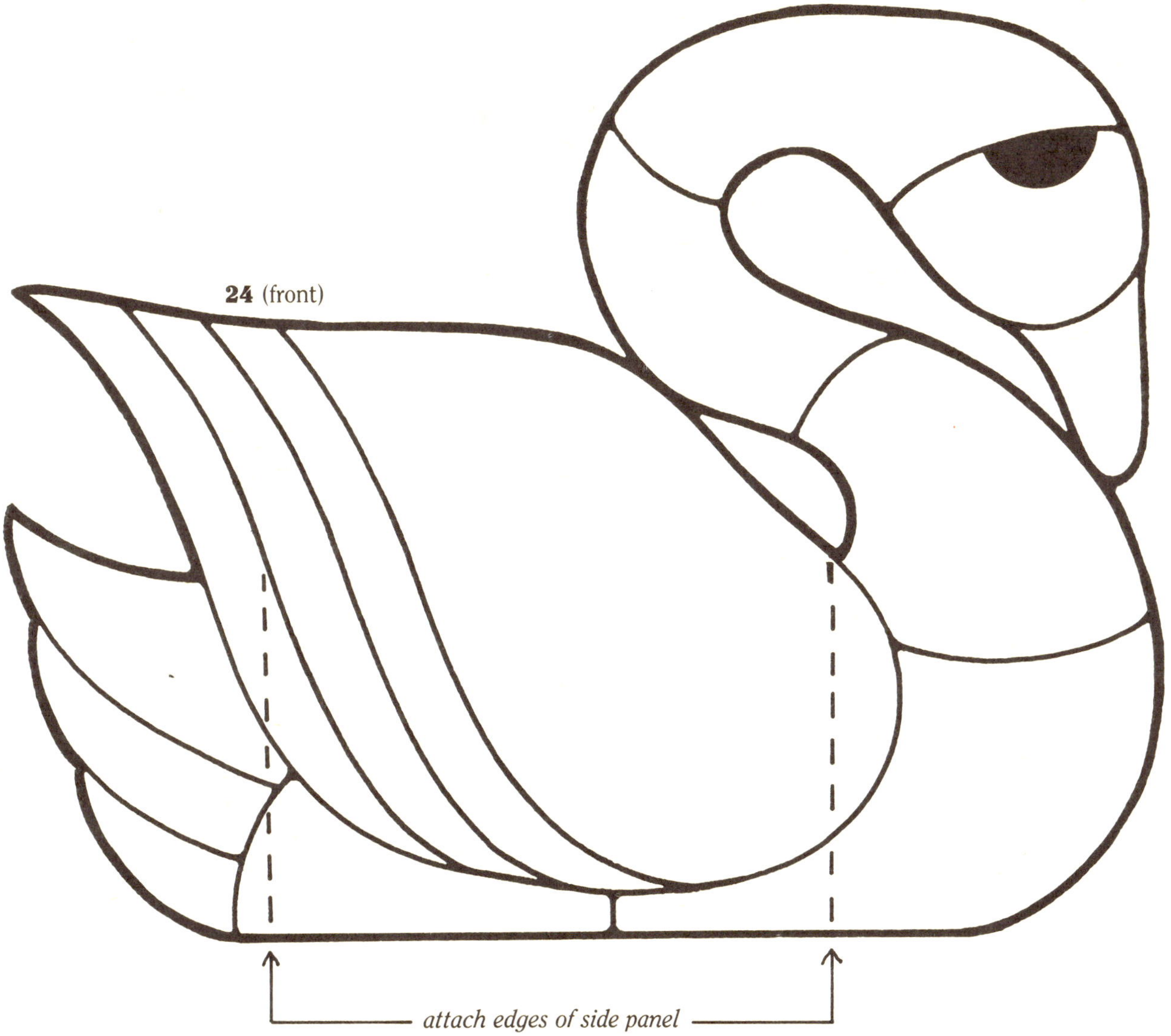

24 (front)

attach edges of side panel

24 (side)

PLATE 18

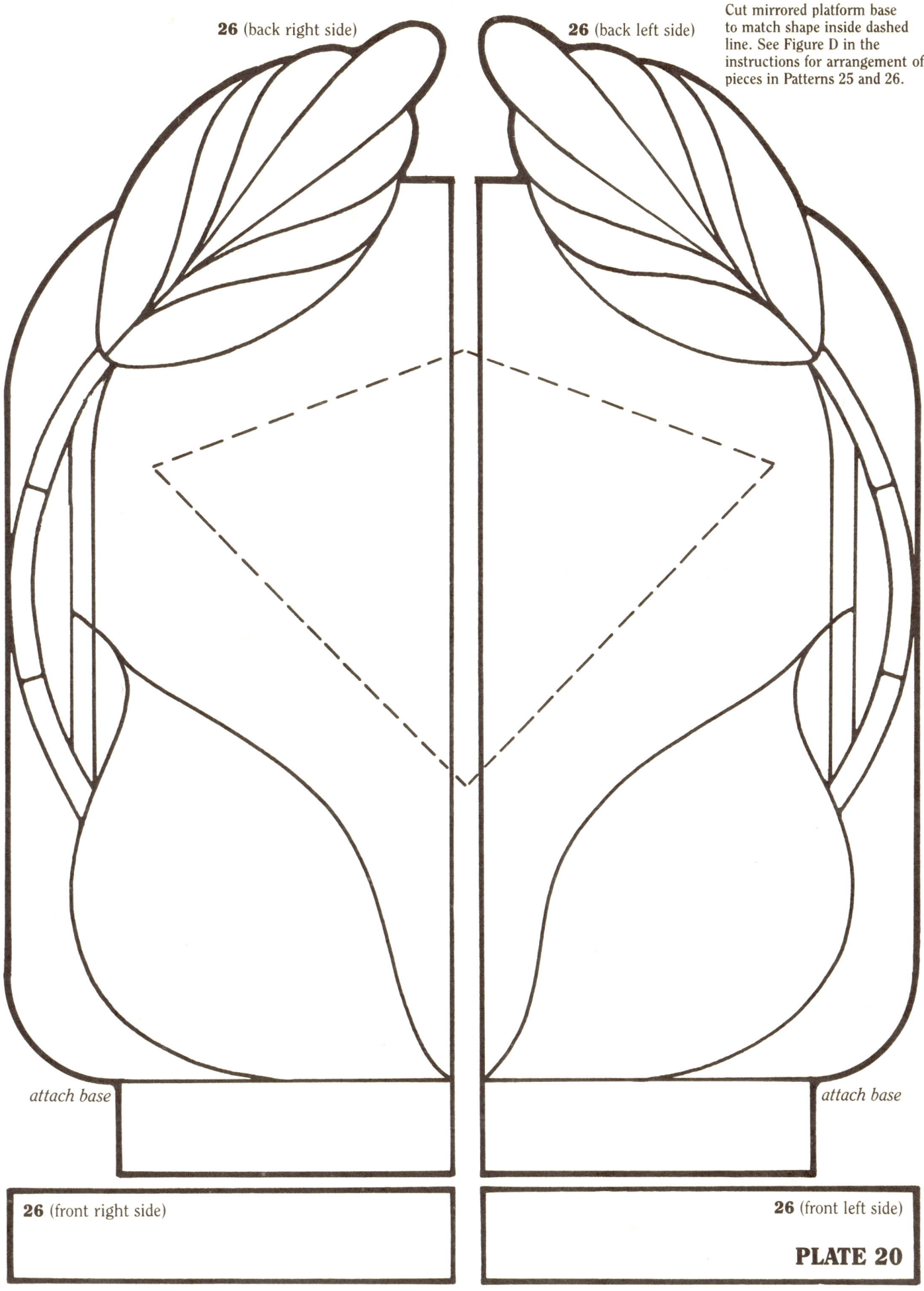

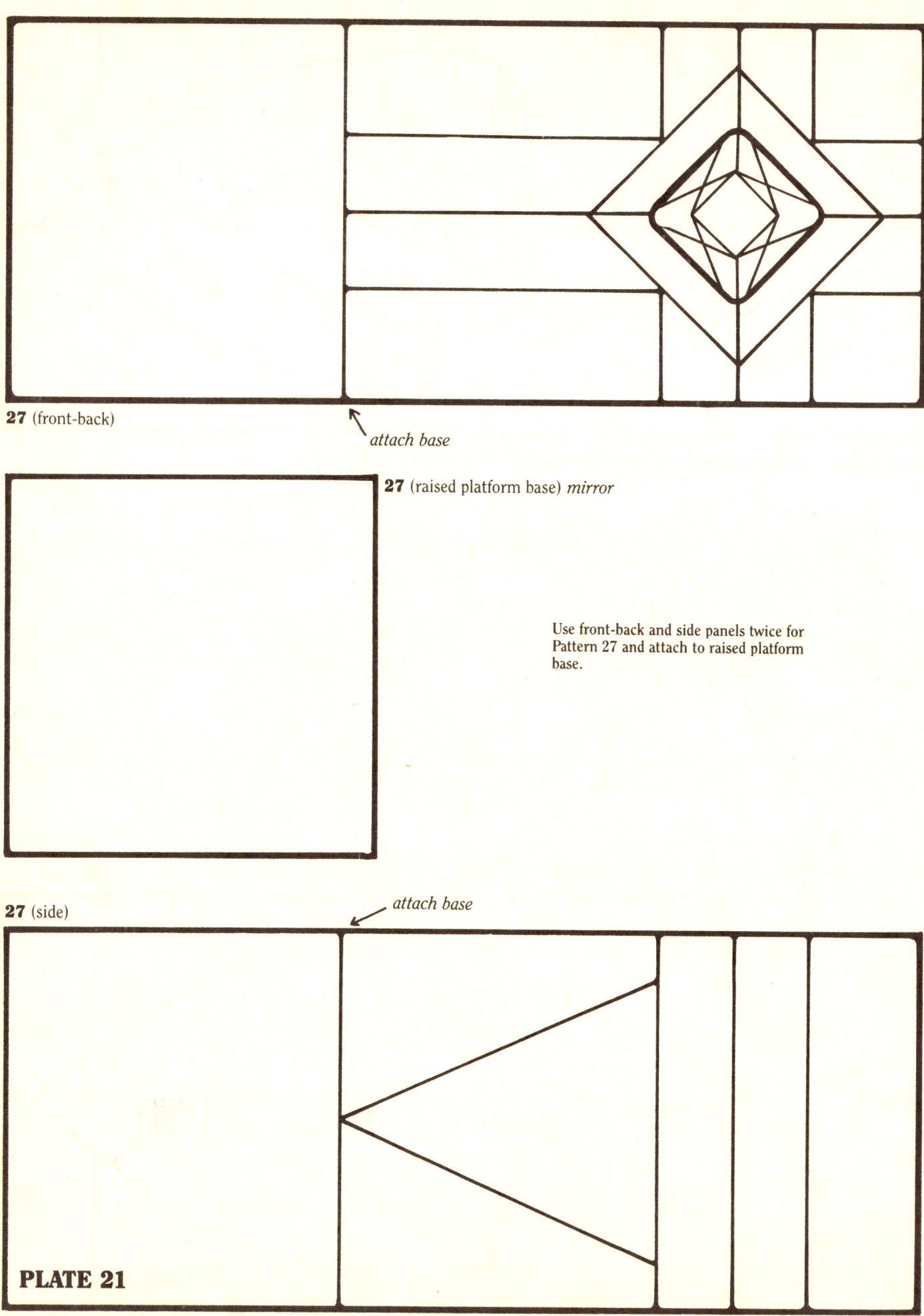

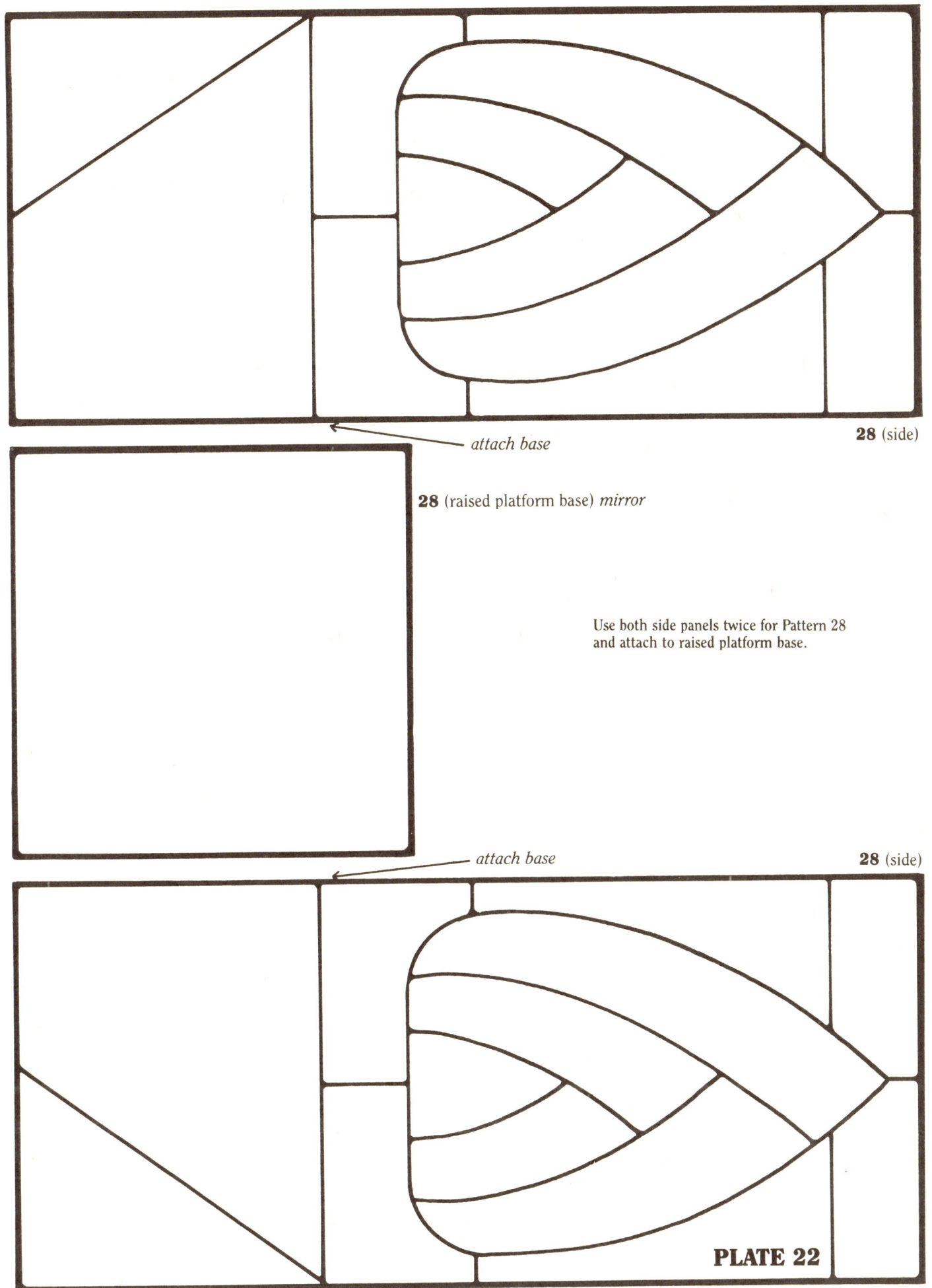

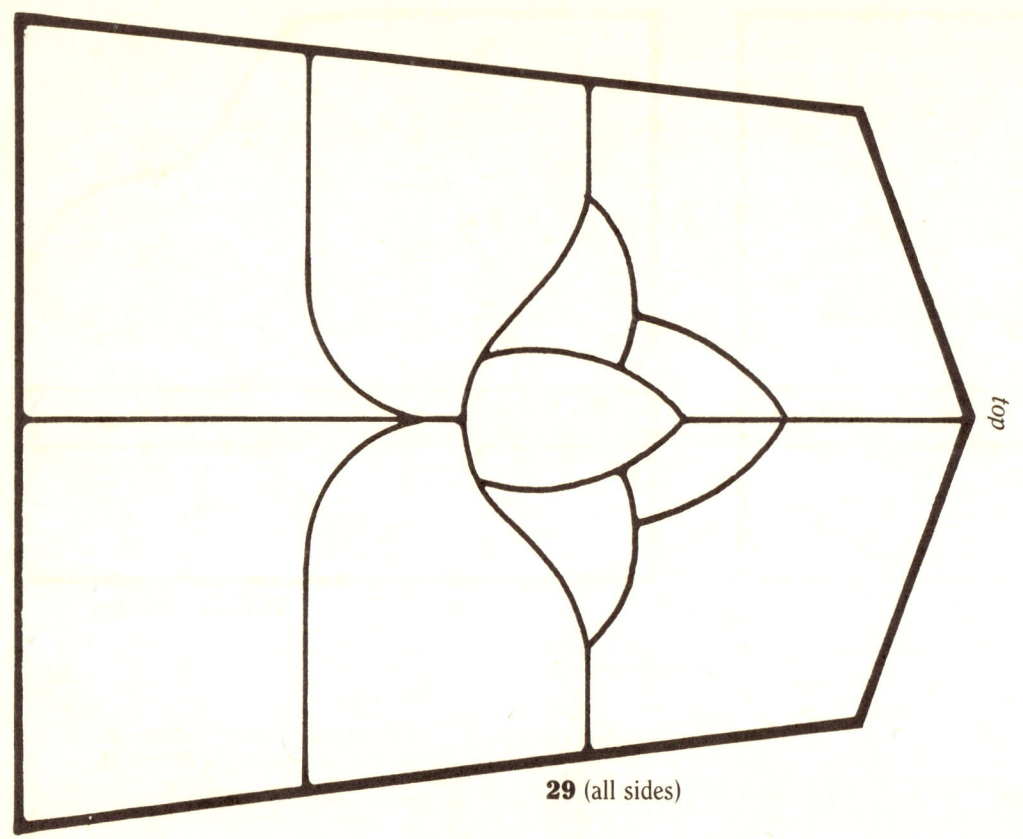

29 (all sides)

Use side panel four times for Patterns 29 and 30.

30 (all sides)

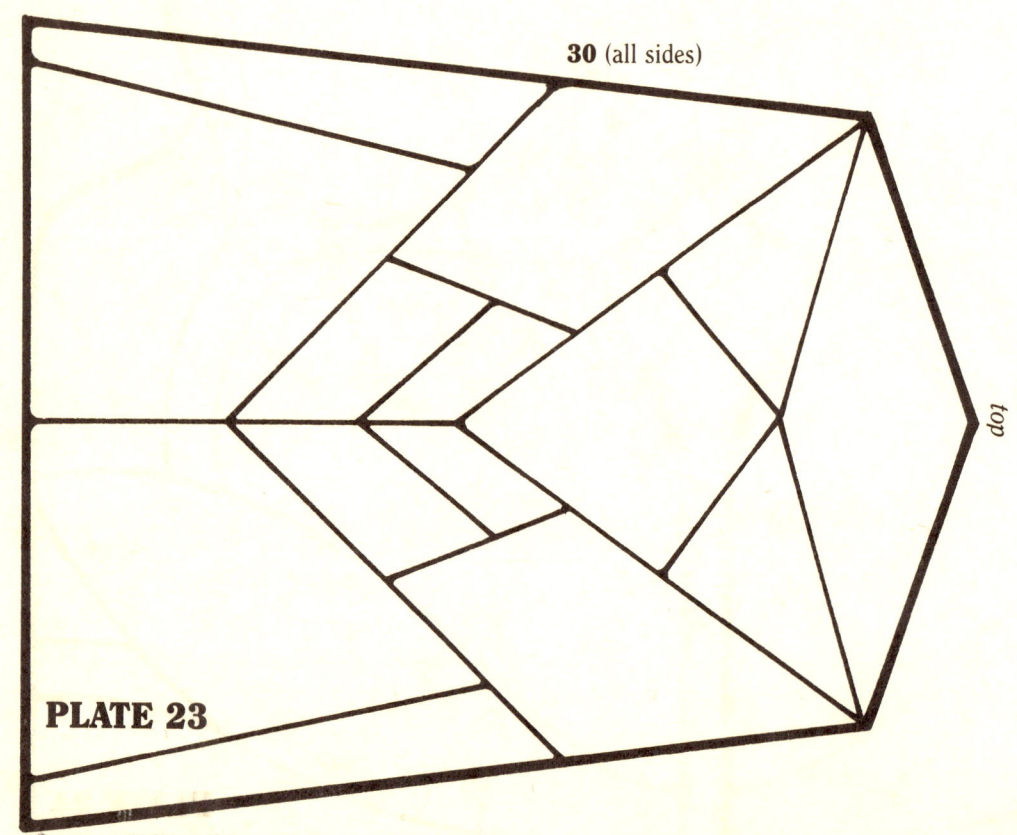

PLATE 23

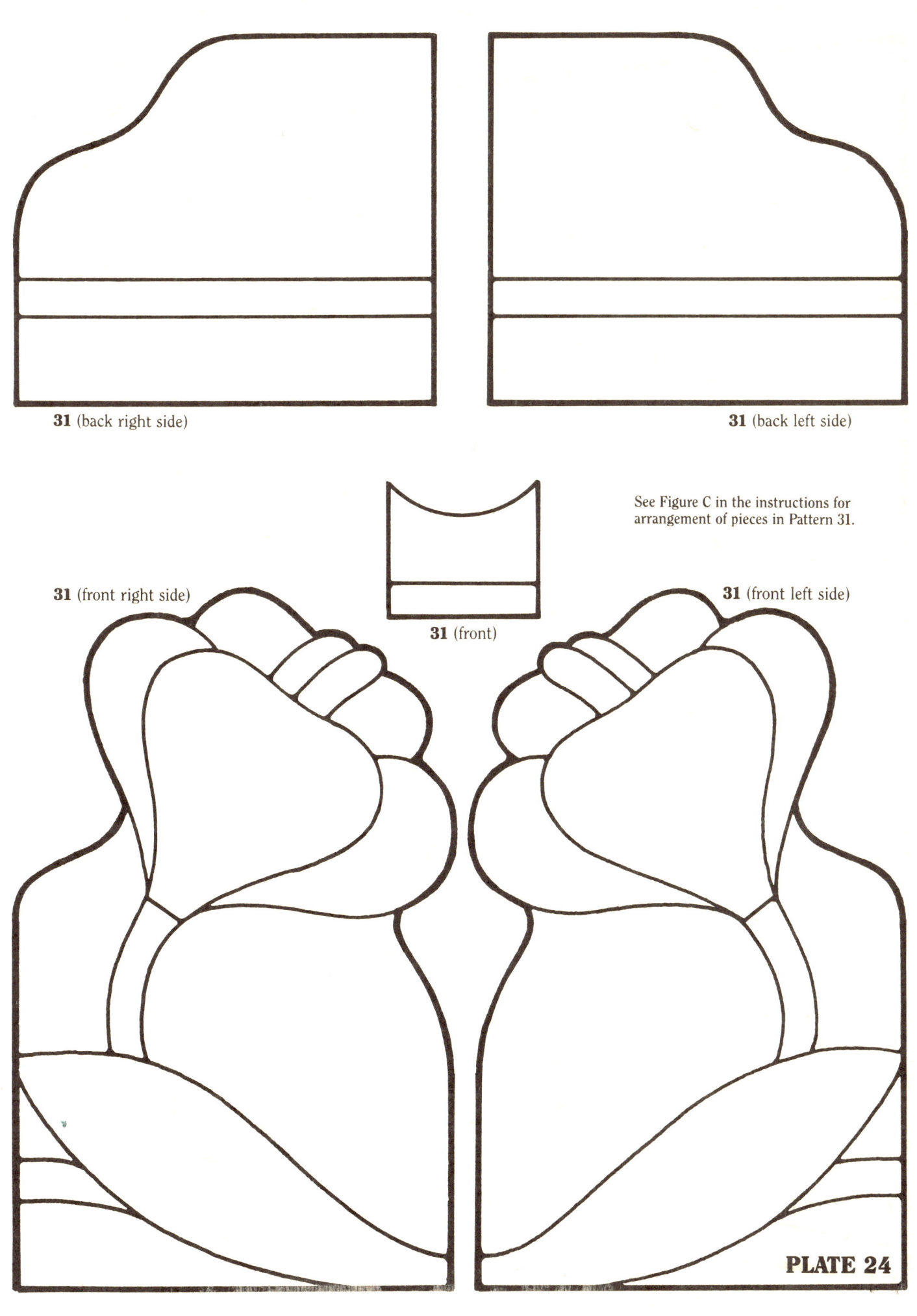

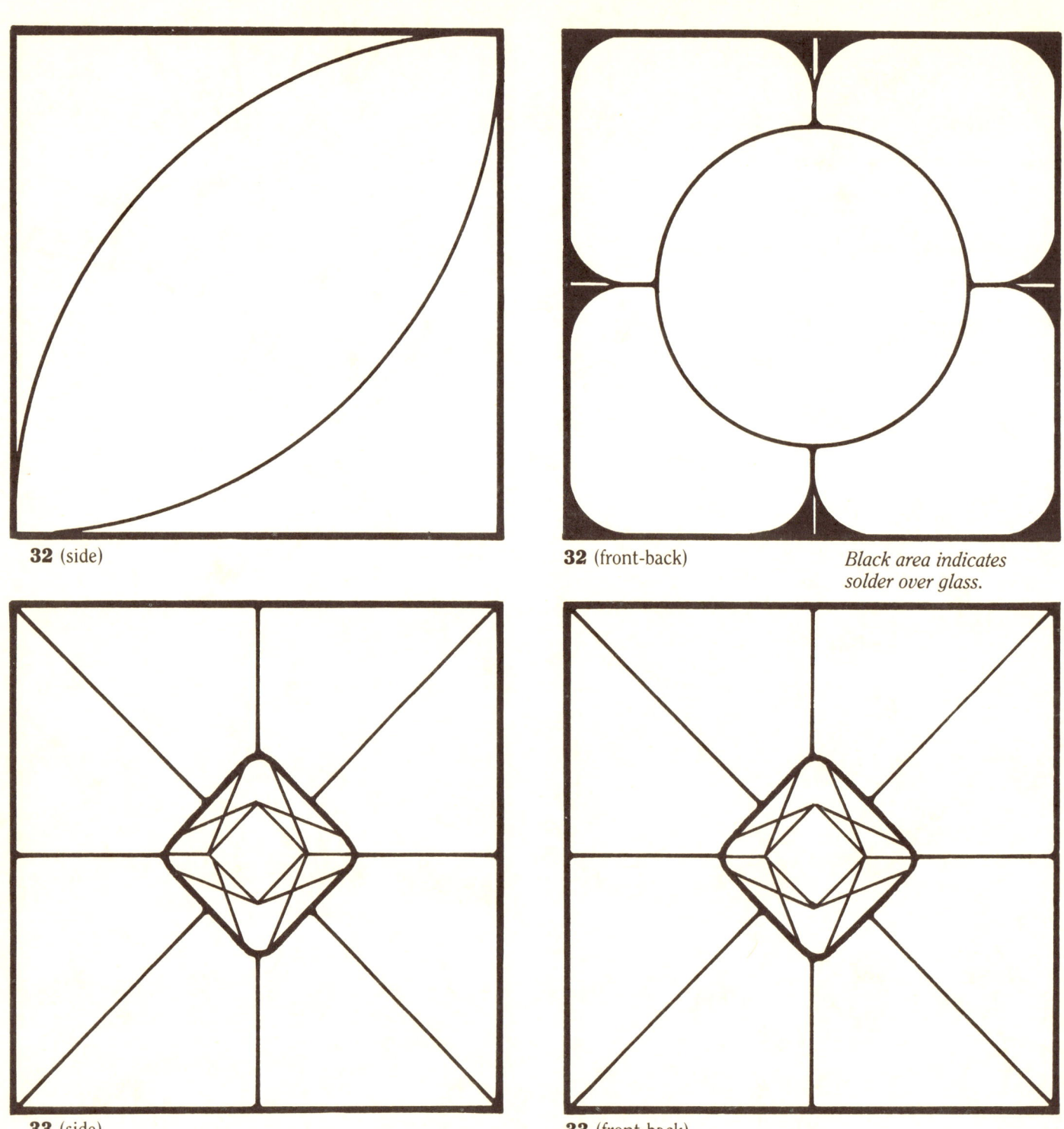

32 (side)

32 (front-back)   *Black area indicates solder over glass.*

33 (side)

33 (front-back)

Use front-back and side panels twice for Patterns 32 and 33.

PLATE 25

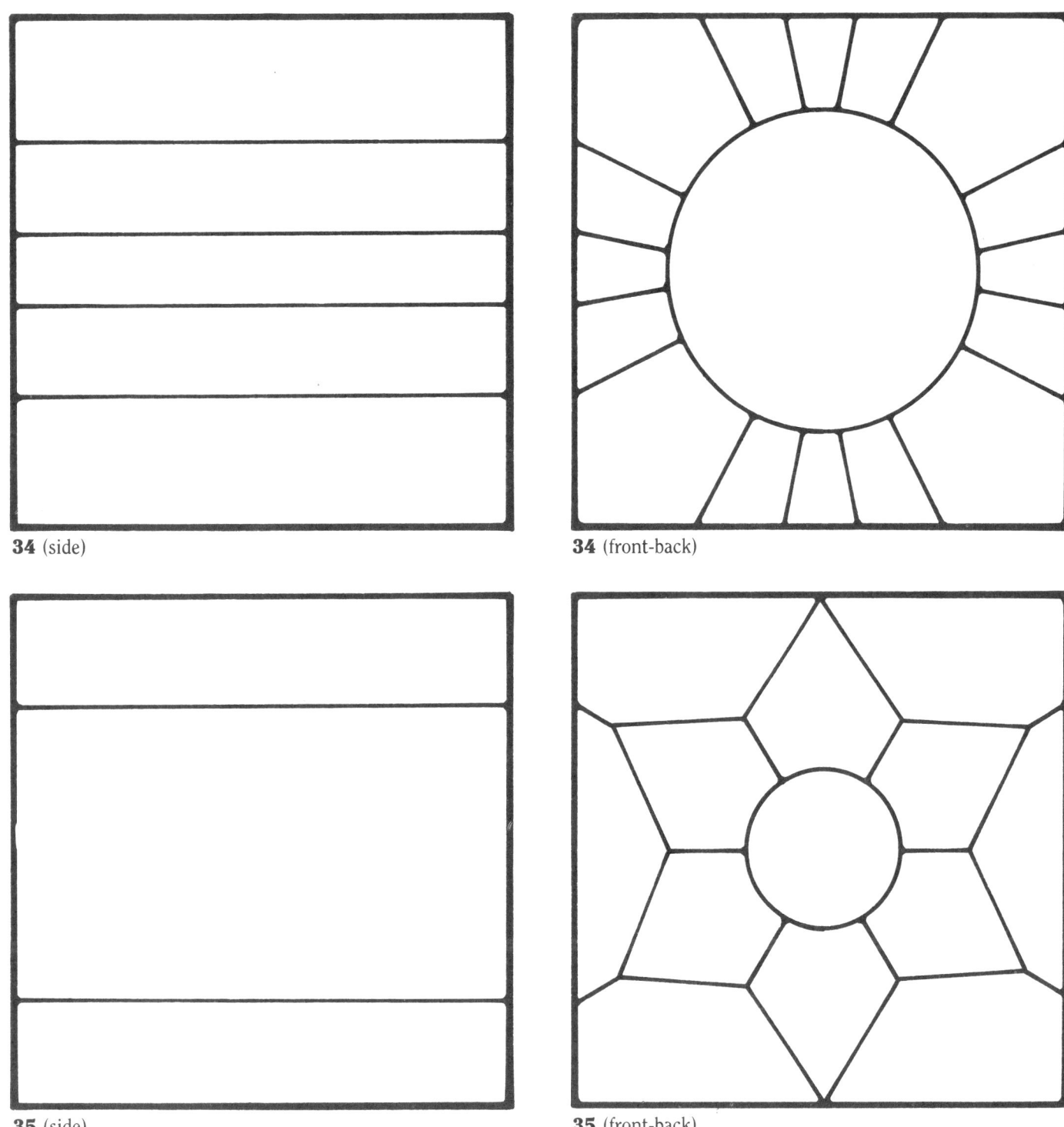

34 (side)

34 (front-back)

35 (side)

35 (front-back)

Use front-back and side panels twice for Patterns 34 and 35.

PLATE 26

36 (front)

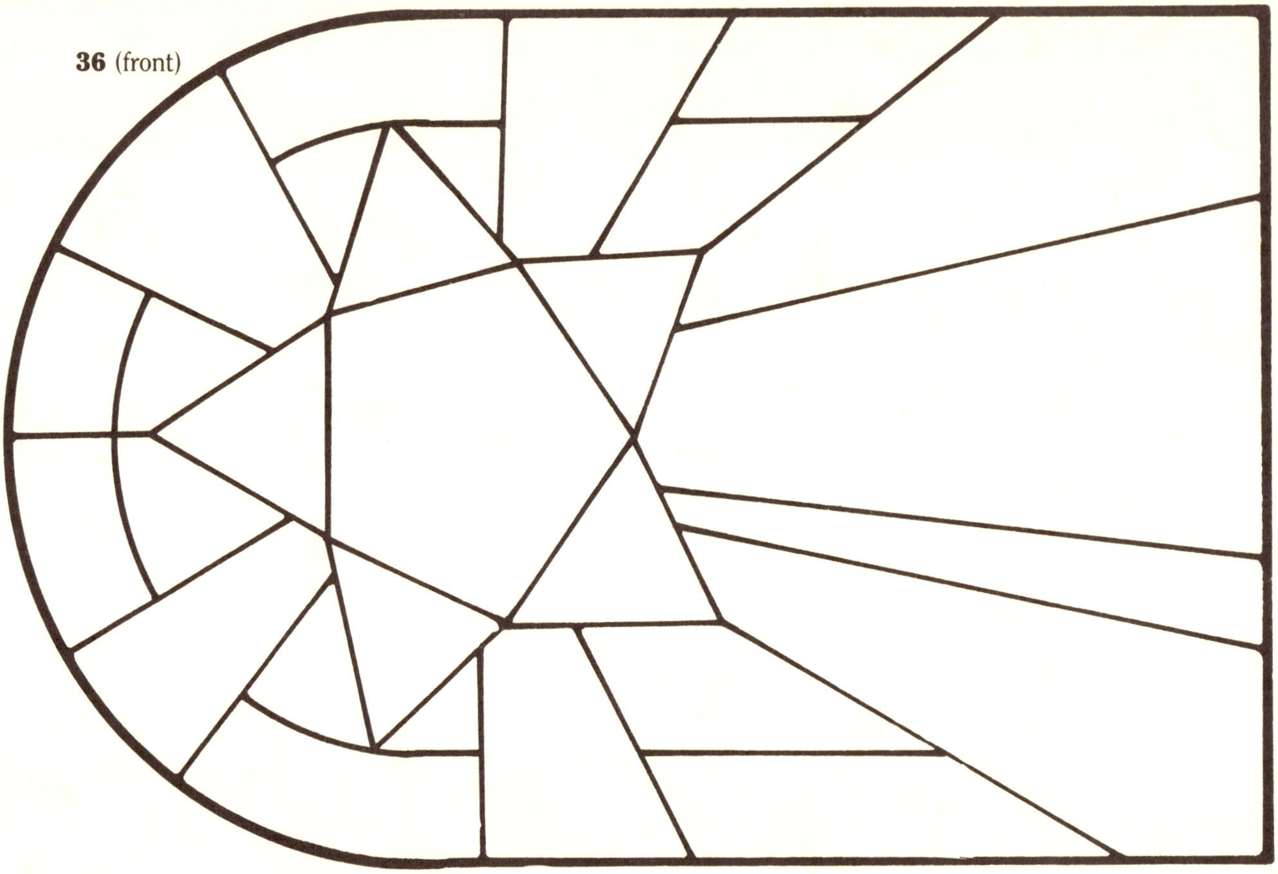

See Figure H in the instructions for arrangement of pieces in Pattern 36.

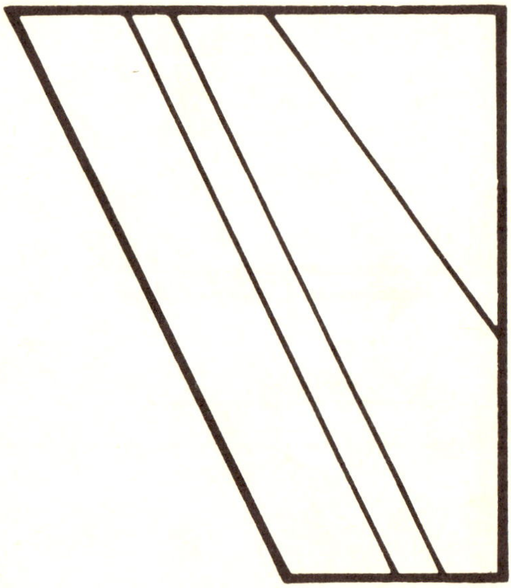

36 (back side)

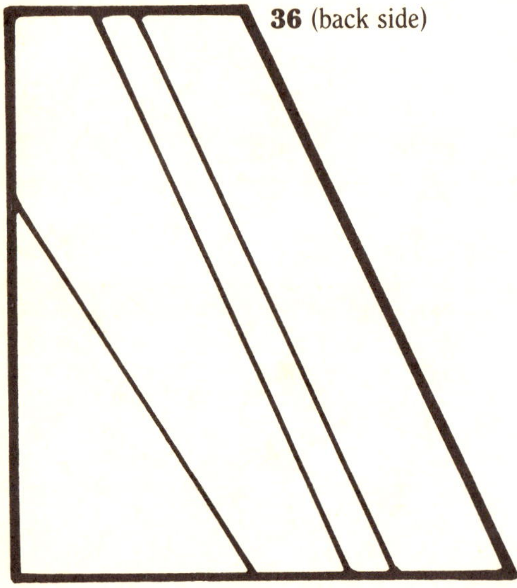

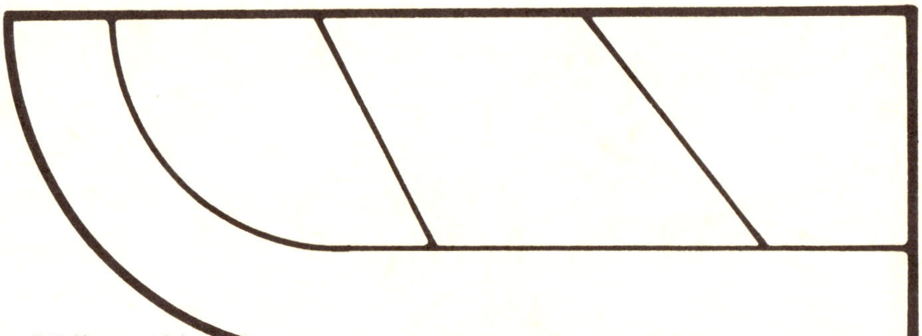

36 (front side)

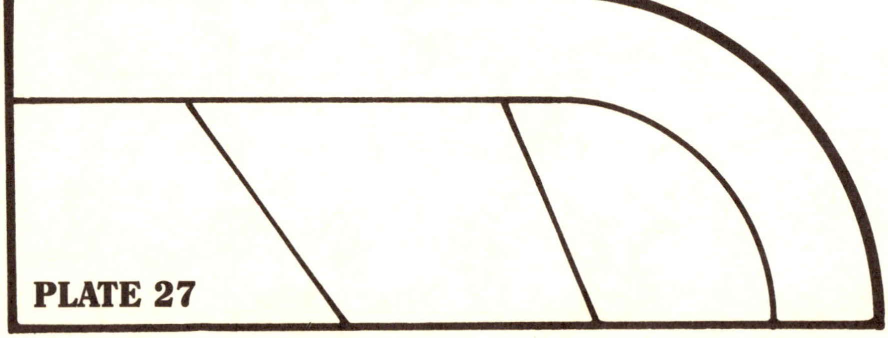

36 (front side)

36 (back side)

PLATE 27

37 (front)

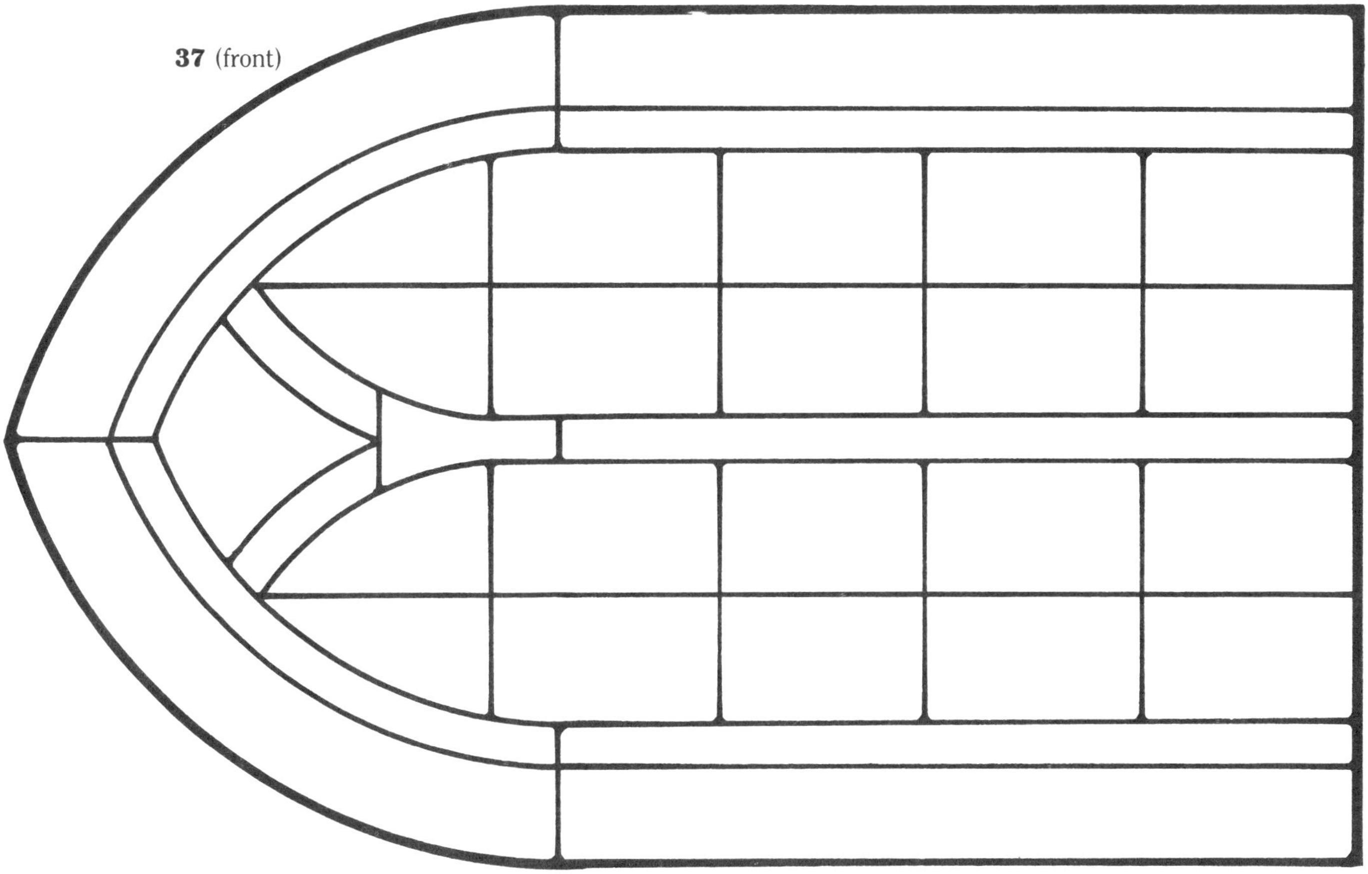

See Figure H in the instructions for arrangement of pieces in Pattern 37.

37 (back side)

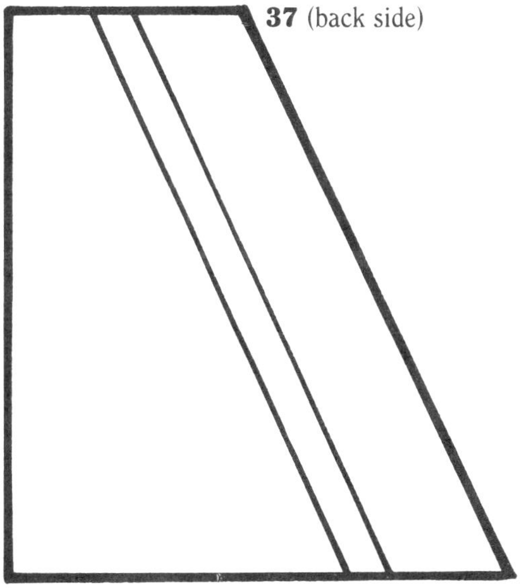

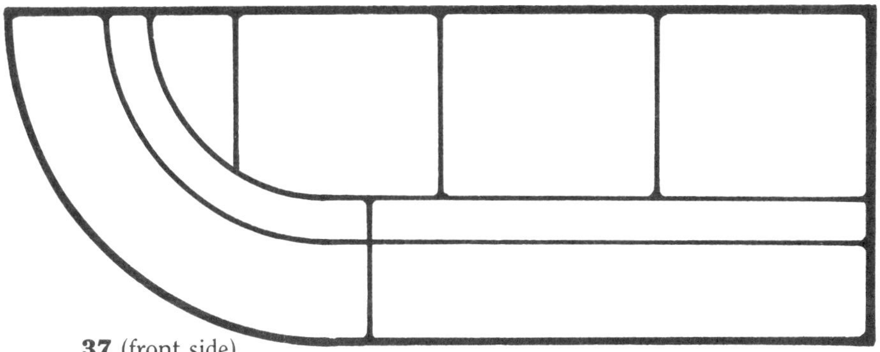

37 (front side)

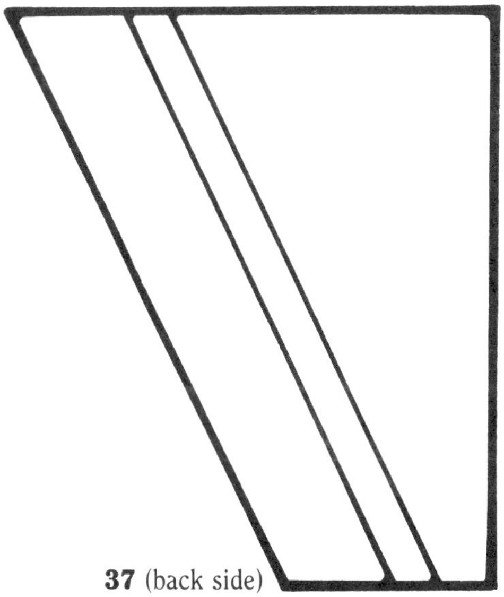

37 (front side)

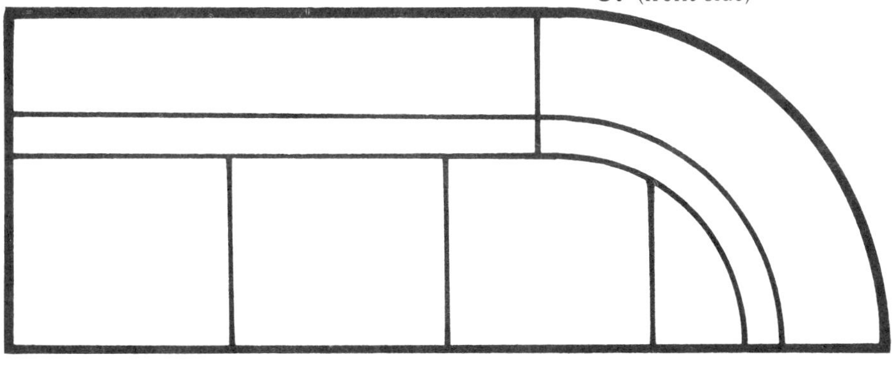

37 (back side)

PLATE 28

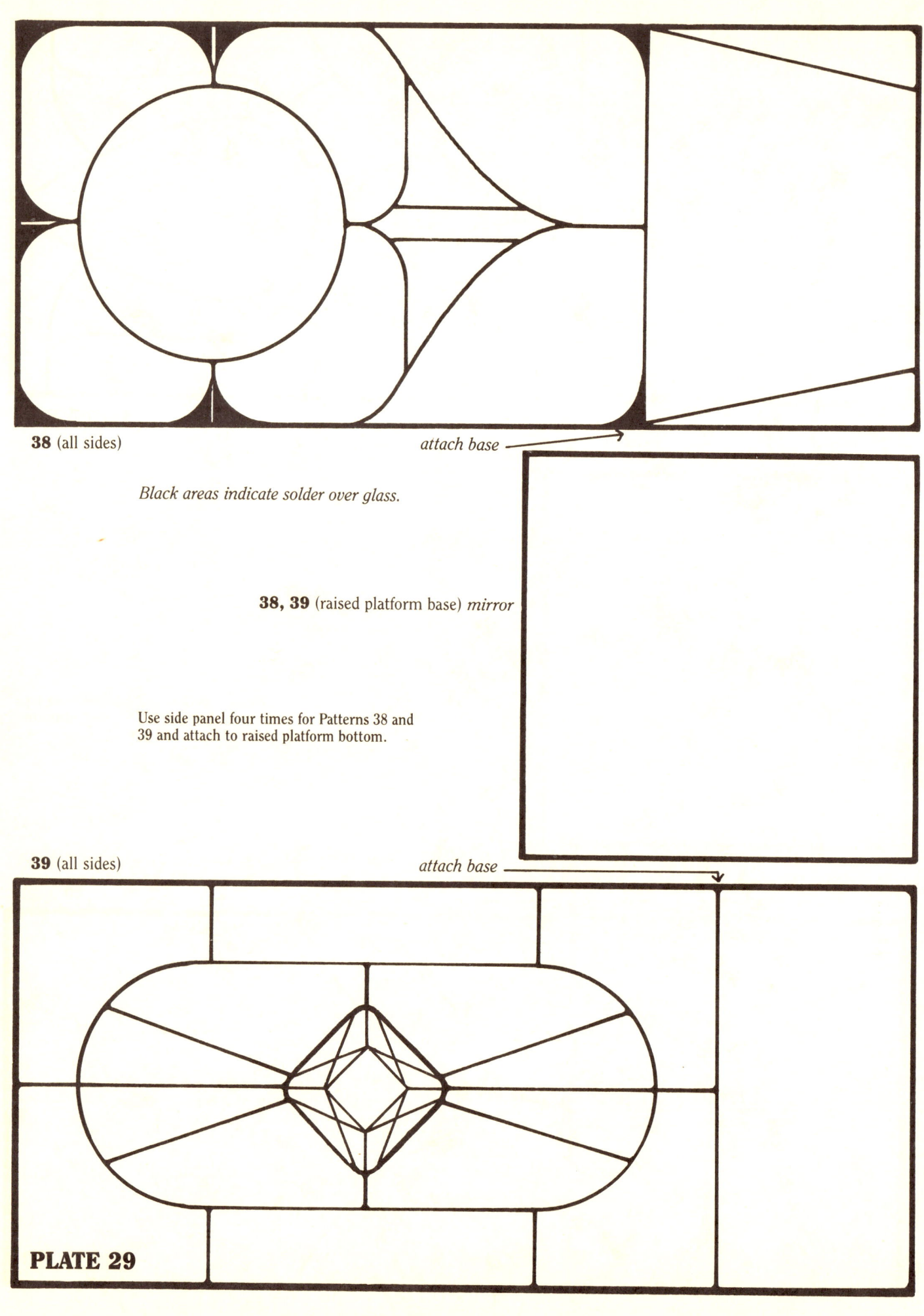

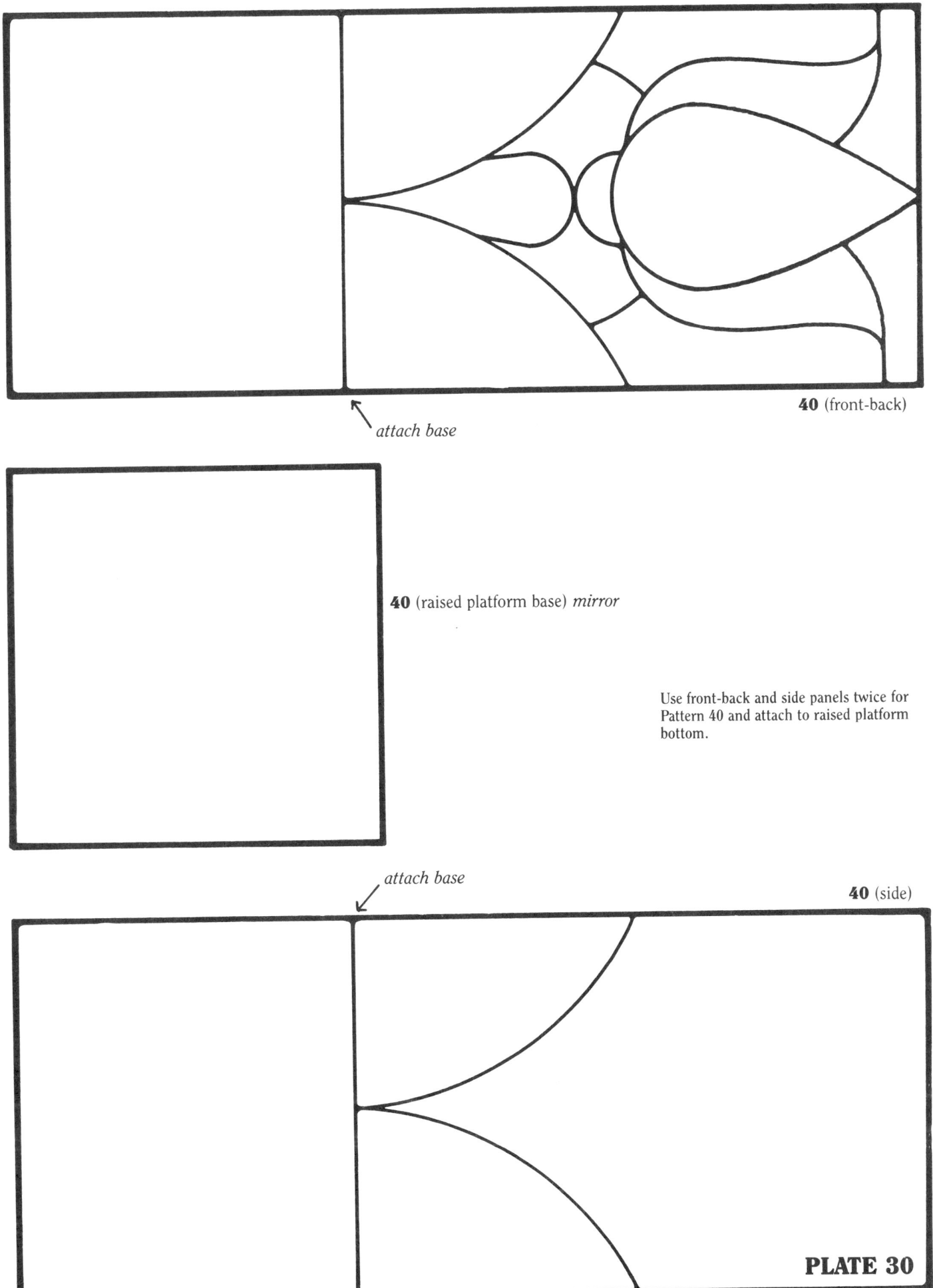

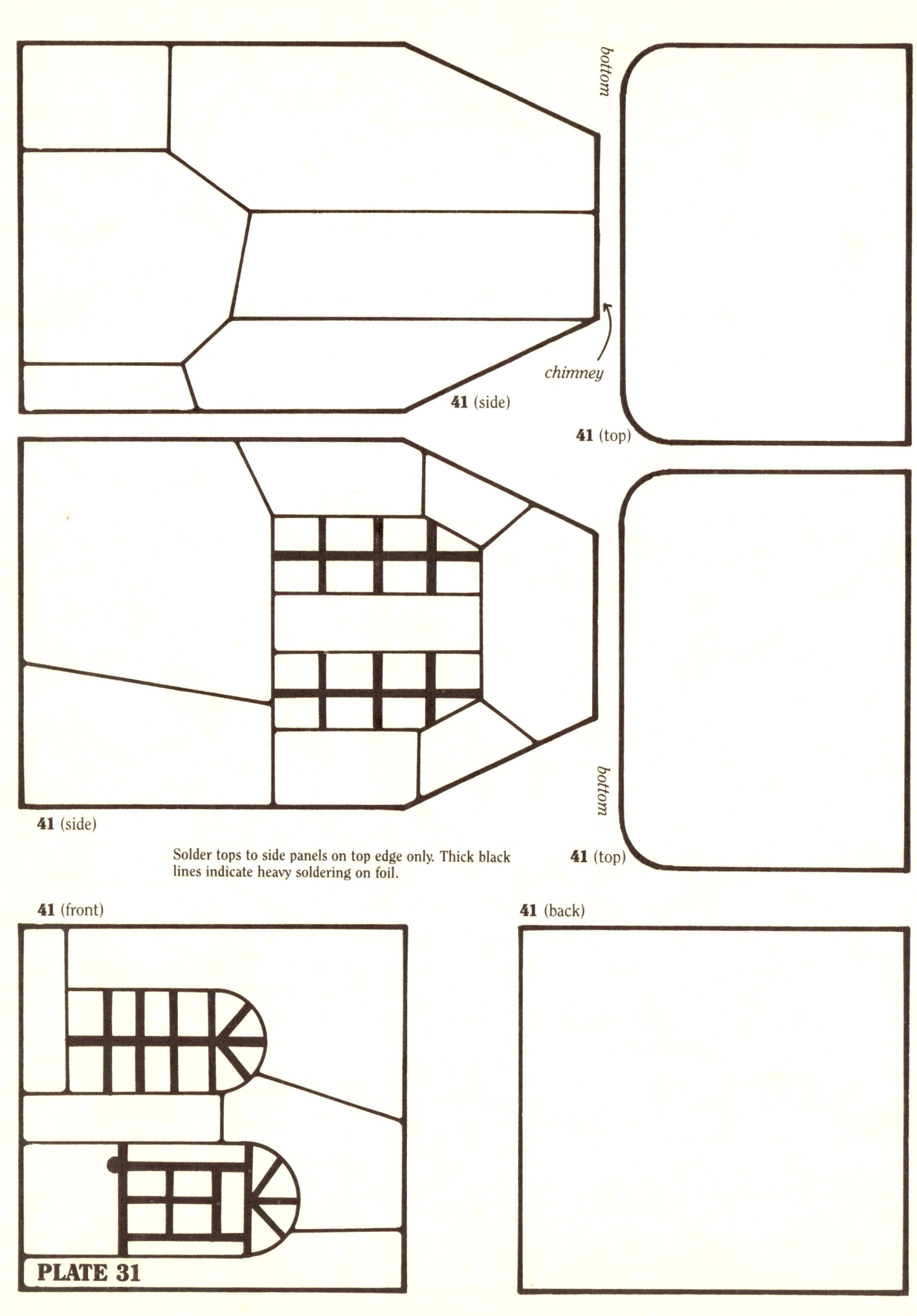

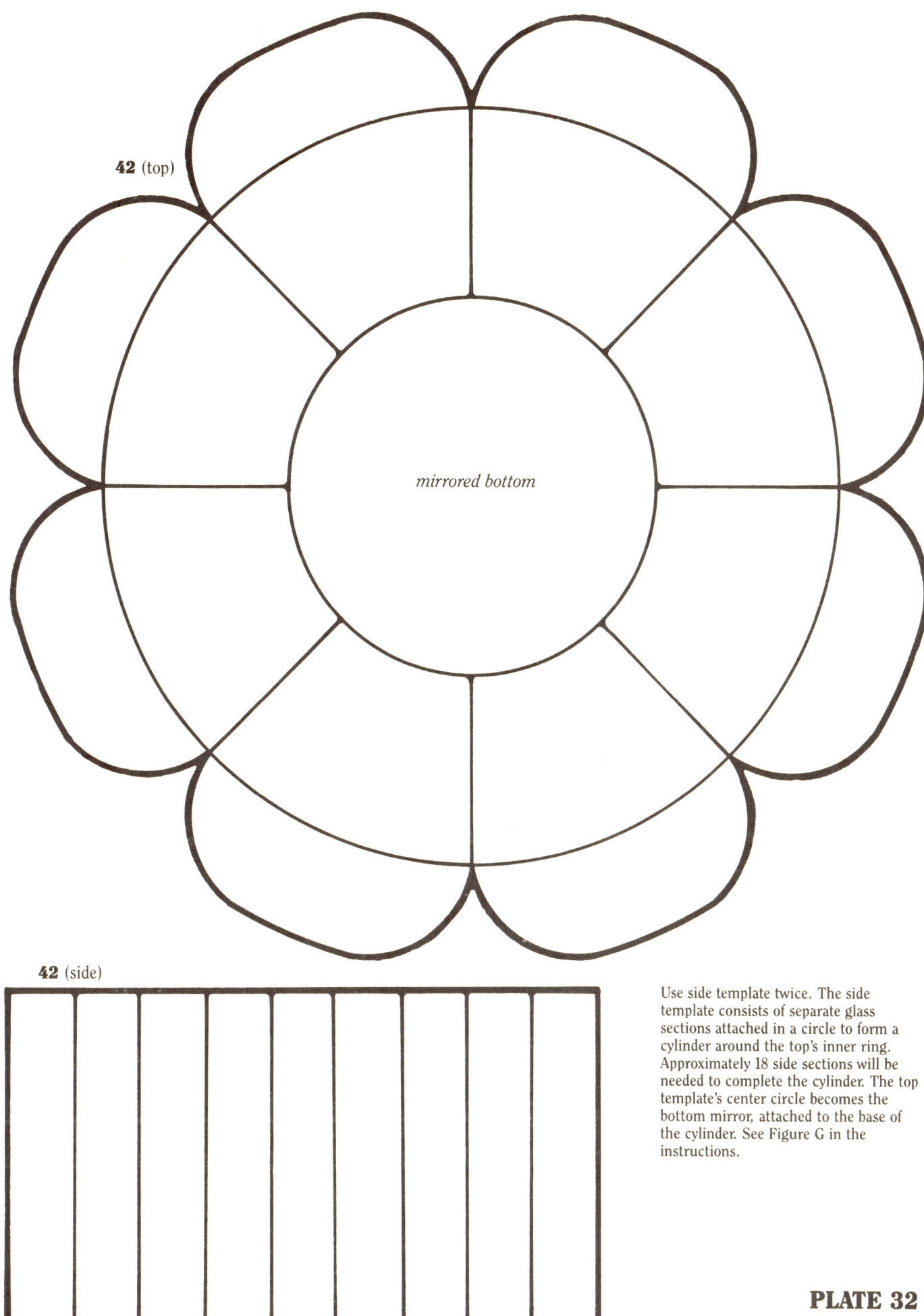

42 (top)

mirrored bottom

42 (side)

Use side template twice. The side template consists of separate glass sections attached in a circle to form a cylinder around the top's inner ring. Approximately 18 side sections will be needed to complete the cylinder. The top template's center circle becomes the bottom mirror, attached to the base of the cylinder. See Figure G in the instructions.

PLATE 32